Also written by Nikki Henderson

Moments with God: Short Stories for the Soul of a Woman

Storm Clouds are Passing: Hold on Until Change Comes

MY GREATEST
Blessings

MEMOIRS *of a* SINGLE MOM

NIKKI HENDERSON

Foreword by Pauline Henderson

WESTBOW
PRESS®
A DIVISION OF THOMAS NELSON
& ZONDERVAN

This book is a work of non-fiction. Unless otherwise noted, the author and the publisher make no explicit guarantees as to the accuracy of the information contained in this book and in some cases, names of people and places have been altered to protect their privacy.

WestBow Press books may be ordered through booksellers or by contacting:

WestBow Press
A Division of Thomas Nelson & Zondervan
1663 Liberty Drive
Bloomington, IN 47403
www.westbowpress.com
1 (866) 928-1240

Scripture quotations are taken from the Holy Bible, New Living Translation, copyright © 1996, 2004, 2007 by Tyndale House Foundation. Used by permission of Tyndale House Publishers, Inc., Carol Stream, Illinois 60188. All rights reserved.

ISBN: 978-1-9736-9280-5 (sc)
ISBN: 978-1-9736-9281-2 (hc)
ISBN: 978-1-9736-9279-9 (e)

Library of Congress Control Number: 2020909757

Print information available on the last page.

WestBow Press rev. date: 06/17/2020

To My Sons, Joshua and Jeremiah, whom I love with all my heart.
When God gave me you, it was the greatest blessing I could ever receive.

To my mother and all parents – your strength and
courage shines forth for all the world to see.

CONTENTS

FOREWORD

*Praise the Lord, all you nations; extol him, all
you peoples. For great is his love toward us, and
the faithfulness of the Lord endures forever.
Praise the Lord
—Psalms 117: 1 – 2*

God has been faithful, and I have surely seen his merciful kindness
from the time that Nikki came into the world. Through hardship
and pain, God has been with us and kept us. I have seen God raise
Nikki up, and I have always seen the talent within her. I noticed
from the time she was a baby; she would stand in front of the
television in Germany to entertain our family friends while we
were in the military. She didn't even speak English yet! We did not
always understand her German language, but I always knew there
was something about her that was special. I predicted she would be
a speaker, writer, or a lawyer.

As I have watched Nikki grow as a writer and speaker and her
heart for God, God spoke to me to let me know she is called to share
a Rhema "Now" word. She is here for this time now. I admonish
Nikki to continue to be excellent in her walk with the Lord and
aspire for greatness in all she is called to do. She is drawn to touch
lives, and healing of broken hearts will come through her work and
ministry.

Being a single mother myself and raising three girls, one of the things my mother taught me was to be an independent woman, trust God, and rely on Him to be your strength. She taught me how to be strong and not put my dependency on anyone else except God. I have been able to be steadfast in raising my children. There were some difficult times. Fathers were there, but the bulk of the work was on me. But I always taught my children to love their father despite my singleness. I always instill positive thoughts and love. The strength of our family was love. I found strength in my mother, father, brother, cousins, aunts, and the list goes on. My family support was the greatest gift in helping me raise my children. From Jamaica, West Indies to Bronx, New York, they have been my strength.

Love is the most significant key in being a parent — single or married. The love you show your children, the love you extend to others, and, most of all, your love for God is so valuable. And don't forget about the love God has for you. As you read this book, it will encourage mothers and fathers as they raise their children. Single parenting is not easy, but Nikki writes this book as a reminder that you are not single – you always have a Father who is there with you, Your Eternal Father. So, sit back, relax, and enjoy the journey as Nikki shares her experiences, lessons, and reflections. May it warm your soul and keep the continuous fire of love burning within all who encounter it.

Pauline Henderson, Nikki's Mom

PREFACE

When you sit to write a book that accounts for life's journey, there is a vulnerability that can cause the pen to pause. Yet, the desire to share and impact pushes the pen to write again. This book embodies three themes: love, family, and faith. It serves as an account of the miraculous blessings of my miracles – my two children. And then the journey of raising them as a single mom over this past decade. I have carried this book for many years as I lived through the pages in my heart. I admit that I could not fit it all in this one book. Some memories would not resurface – and I did not force them. Instead, I allowed the flow of transparency and love to infuse onto these pages as they wished.

The photograph that graces this cover was the spark that ignited my fire to share my heart and story. As my sons look to me to be the strong woman that stands as an example in their life, I humbly look forward. I absolutely enjoyed my season of finally writing this book. There were tears on some pages as I extracted from deep crevices of my soul. There were laughs on other pages as I recalled lessons and made light of them. Throughout this book, deep thought caused me to reflect in ways I had never done before. I wrote this book in between sleeping hours and in my dreams. I am humbled by every moment you utilize to read these pages ahead, and I provide you my time-guarantee that it will be a blessing to you. My qualification to write this work does not necessarily rest in specific titles or fields. Instead, it rests in love and transparency.

It rests in my acknowledgment of the blessings God has graced me with. Upon completion of this work, I feel emotionally naked and unashamed. My desire is that this book will allow light to shine forth – in you and me.

ACKNOWLEDGMENTS

*In all thy ways acknowledge him, and
he shall direct your paths.*
—Proverbs 3:6

First, I must acknowledge God, who directed my path before I entered this world. Even when I have gone astray, like a loving Father, He redirects me to the path I must take. Father, thank you for another opportunity to pour words out onto the pages. Thank you for your inspiration and thank you for loving me.

To my babies, Joshua and Jeremiah, my sons; You both belong to God and are on loan to me here on this earth. I love you more than words, and I pray these pages will remain a legacy for you. I want to let the world know how much I love you and what it means to have you both in my life. I also wanted to share the lessons you have taught me. May you become the amazing Men that God has ordained you to be, and my heart desire is that I can see it.

To my mother, Pauline, my love, and best girlfriend (smile); You allowed your life to be an open book for me and my sisters so we could learn how to strive despite our circumstances. You are the pages in this book and beyond. You still teach us how to renew, rejuvenate, and recover. I learned how to pray, listening to you on your knees. You are the embodiment of a single mother who took hold of life through love, family, and faith and made the best of it all.

To my father, Super Grandpa, I will always see an "S" on your chest as you swooped into my life and stood as a dedicated father (any many times as a friend). You have supported my sons and me unconditionally. If I could have included you in my picture, I would have you standing there right behind us. You got our back, and I love you for it – always.

To all my family and friends – I appreciate all your love and support over this past decade. Some of you used your hand and words to lift my chin when I held my head down. I am forever indebted to you in love. To my two sisters, Taisha and Nakima - you listen, and you tell me the truth. Thank you for your love and honesty and for always holding your judgment so you could demonstrate your support. To my beautiful nieces and nephews, you are the extension of my story. You are precious, and I am honored to be your aunt.

To all those who will read this book – thank you in advance for your support, and the precious time you will use to digest these words. I pray it will be an inspiration…always.

Sincerely,
Nikki Henderson

INTRODUCTION

In December 2019, I walked across the stage to receive my master's degree in Business Administration. There was an initial hooding ceremony that was personalized to our degrees and gave our families an up-close and personal view. My family had flown in the night before from New York and New Jersey to be apart of this day with me. I wasn't feeling the greatest and had a slight case of laryngitis, but I was determined to attend my graduation - even if I could only whisper. As everyone sat there, I looked out at my two sons, and I could see they were proud of their mom. It was the first time I had the opportunity to attend a graduation. Surely it was a proud day!

After the initial hooding ceremony, we took pictures together as a family and headed over to the main ceremony in the gym. It was packed with people and keeping my head straight; I looked all around to spot my family. Thankfully, my youngest sister wore a red dress that day, so she was easily found among all the black and blue suits. They looked lovingly down at me and gave me a thumbs up and I took my seat to prepare for this much-awaited ceremony.

Then, a defining moment came that I did not expect. The Dean of the University stood up and began to acknowledge our entire class of 2020 — undergraduate and graduate students. It was what he said next that hit me. He recognized that many students had to beat the odds to get there. I nodded with agreement thinking about undergraduate students who had to leave their homes to be alone in a new place. Some military students juggled coursework while on duty. He began to ask students to stand, and he said, "All Single

Parents, please stand." I froze for a moment to let it settle in and embrace that I was getting ready to tell the entire stadium that I was a single mom by simply raising from my seat. My heart raced, and my legs trembled a bit as I rose from my chair. Our Dean continued, "You juggled home and worked to do this, you beat the odds!" and as I stood, I realized it was the proudest moment of my life, and a single tear ran down my face. It was at that moment that I knew I had to write this book. I had to tell my story of how I made it and are still making it over. We come in all shapes and sizes. Some of us are single moms by choice, others are single moms by force, but in the end, we are all precious in God's sight. That day my Dean only acknowledged single parents and students in the military. I am sure many pushed to get to that big day, but rarely had I seen single parents called out and defined, and I felt it was a special moment for me – and for us.

"I didn't ask for this." I have repeated those words in my mind numerous times as I sat with my sons in an empty home. I did not ask to be a statistic. Where was my white picket fence? Where was my little dog barking in the distance? Where was my perfect husband coming home at 6:00 p.m. every day with an empty lunchbox, hungry for his next meal? Where was my ideal situation? Where had I missed it? For many years, I thought my status as a single mom was a misfortune. Not that my children were the misfortune – instead, my condition. But over time, I realized that it was all my greatest blessings. It is my gift and my calling.

This book is meant to encourage you and allow us to celebrate our greatest blessing! I will share experiences and life lessons that I hope will make you laugh, cry, reflect, and start fresh as you read the words of this book. My intention in this book is not to condone or intensify any relational breakdowns. I am a strong advocate for marriage and a two-parent household. I think it is an extreme blessing when it is healthy. On the other end, I embrace the reality that there are times that the story is not written that way and parents must stand in singular units to raise children. Regardless of our story,

I believe strongly in the institution of the family. We should make all efforts to live to the best of our ability for ourselves and our children.

Through this book, I want to share some of my journey and encouragement for those who parent together, and especially those who parent alone. We exist across this world in many cultures, races, and income levels. After eleven years of single parenting, I still must find my way each day. There is no cookie-cutter situation because all kids are different. All mothers and fathers are different. All co-parenting situations vary! We all have different roads to travel, but we all have one thing in common – our greatest blessings!

Children are a gift from the Lord;
they are a reward from him.
—Psalms 127:3

Merriam-Webster Dictionary has several definitions for the word blessing. Blessing is the act or words of one that blesses. For example, someone may say a blessing over their food or someone else. Blessing is also an approval or encouragement. When a man approaches a woman's father and asks for her hand in marriage, he is seeking a "blessing" from the woman's father. While all these definitions were relatable – there was one definition that stood out to me and tapped my heartstrings. Blessings are also defined as something conducive to happiness or welfare. The word conducive in this context means something that tends to promote or assist. In other words, blessings are parts of our lives that encourage or assist us with happiness or welfare.

Now, I had to take you on this word journey because as you walk through this book, I want the theme of blessing to be embedded in your heart. My declaration through this work is that my children are my greatest blessing! Not a career, not money, not cars, or houses. No matter how difficult the journey of single parenting may be, there is a part of this journey that is meant to be a blessing. If you are reading this memoir and are a parent – you could relate to the fact that it hasn't always felt like a blessed journey. There has been difficulty along the way. But as you walk through this book, I seek to pull forward the immense joy and blessing the journey brings. At the end of this book, there are questions for each chapter to help foster internal reflection and discussion.

If you are reading this memoir but are not a parent – please remain present for the entire journey. I believe that there are areas of our lives that are common ground – we all have blessings in our lives. For some of us, our greatest blessing may be a mother or a father. It may be a sibling or a friend. It may even be a stranger. The point of the matter is that once you identify those moments and individuals in your life, it is a significant breakthrough because it will ultimately change your perception of where you have been and where you are going.

1

One More Epi!

*Miracles happen all the time – sometimes it is
just a matter of how we recognize them.*

I didn't start out as a single mom. At a young age, I was married to a guy I met at church. It was love at first sight with a wedding just one year later to the date. I always desired to be married and have children amongst all my other ambitions. About one year into the marriage, we realized that pregnancy was not happening as soon as we thought. As a matter of fact, it ended up being seven years before I gave birth to my first child. During those seven years, my marriage was rocky. A lot of ebbs and flows and ups and downs, but we wanted to prove to ourselves and the world that we didn't make a mistake by walking down the aisle. So, we stuck it out. I stuck it out for ten years, to be exact. Looking back, I do not know how the time went by so fast yet so slow at the same time. But enough of that - let me tell you how I got my precious Joshua.

At around the sixth year, we decided we would take the step of seeing an infertility doctor. It was a humbling step, and it was also the next logical progression for us since the pregnancy was not happening naturally. I can remember being nervous and going to the visit that day with my head held down. Infertility plays on the emotions and can consume you if you focus on why you are not fruitful. The meeting with the doctor was all a blur. He told us about

1

the steps we could take, and most of all, we learned how much it would cost (thousands of dollars). We had insurance at the time, but there were some procedures and treatments that were not covered. So not only would we be taking a physical chance, but we would also be considering a financial gamble. We left the doctor's office determined to try. It was all we could do.

Around that time, we had a vacation scheduled to go down to Georgia. My mom had purchased a vacation home there, and we were looking forward to visiting it. It was a beautiful home in a peaceful neighborhood, and I surely needed the getaway. I had a cousin who was moving to Georgia at that same time, and we planned to visit the site of their new home, which was being built. We made it to Georgia and settled in, and before I knew it, we were in contract to build a new home in Georgia as well! We picked out all the details of the flooring and the kitchen. We were ecstatic! That night I went to bed feeling excited about the possibility of starting a new life.

The next morning my husband at that time woke up and said he had a dream. He said that in the dream, his friend from work came into the very room we were in and told him that he was going to have a baby! We laughed at that dream and agreed that it was an odd dream.

That same day we took a trip down to Alabama to visit my grandmother (may God rest her soul — I miss her dearly). We were planning to go to church with her that Sunday, so we spent Saturday checking out the historic Tuskegee, Alabama, sites. The next morning, we went to church. I soaked in the down-home southern preaching that Sunday by a pastor who knew me since I was a little girl. I praised, and I worshipped and danced just like they did.

One aspect of that church I loved so much was the intensity of their intercessory prayer before each service. You could see the entire church come in and kneel at the altar and cry out to God every service — man, woman, young and old. At the end of the service, the pastor called my husband and me forward. I was shocked because that was not his standard protocol, but I also knew he always had me sing a song when I visited. I was known as Momye's granddaughter, Nikki, from New York. I would come down with my northern accent, and they loved to hear it.

We walked up there, and the next few moments were life changing. God miraculously revealed to the pastor that we were considering infertility drugs. I knew it had to be God's leading because I had not yet told anyone in my family what we were thinking. He said that we were not going to need any drugs and that the miracle would happen right then! He called his wife forward, who had given birth to ten children at the time. She proceeded to pray with me intensely. I remember this warm feeling running through me, and I felt God's power through her prayers. Everyone shouted and praised in advance for the miracle. We packed up and headed back to New Jersey after that week, excited about the future. Because I struggled for pregnancy, a part of me was afraid to embrace the faith that had been bestowed on my situation that day. But without faith, it is impossible to please God!

*So Then faith comes by hearing, and
hearing by the word of God.
—Romans 10:17*

I went about life as usual over the next month or so. I suffered from irregular menstrual periods, so it was not a significant point if my menstrual was late. But this time, I felt a little different, and lo and behold within that next month, I was pregnant! The miracle occurred! No drugs, no doctors, just God, and the prayers of those who cared for me dearly!

I was encouraged to find out I was pregnant, and I had my first doctor's visit and saw the little heartbeat. It was so precious — my dream come true! My body was struggling, but my mind was way ahead in the delivery room. Yet, I did not know the journey that was ahead for me. The first obstacle showed up in the form of genetic testing. The doctor advised that there was a chance my child could have severe anemia and asked me if I wanted to decide to keep my baby or terminate since it was still early. I remember taking that call in a conference call at work on my lunch break. My heart dropped immediately. I decided I would move forward, having the faith that my child would be healthy.

The next obstacle showed up in the form of heart palpitations. I would feel my heart beating out of my chest at times. I was losing a pound a day even though I was past the point of morning sickness. A review of my bloodwork determined that I was suffering from hyperthyroidism. Everything was speeding up in my body. I lost my appetite and could barely have a good meal. My mother came and made me one of my favorite Jamaican dishes —stew peas and rice. It was so good, and within minutes it all came up! I remember crying and my mother holding me because I was so upset at that moment.

With all the sickness showing up, I had to cut back at work, and we made the difficult decision to withdraw from the contract on the home in Georgia. The reality was that we would not be able to afford the down payment or the mortgage at the rate my health was going. And we didn't know what the future held. Thankfully the realtor was gracious and allowed us to cancel the home contract with no penalty.

Each day I struggled to feel well, but I enjoyed the thought of my beautiful baby growing inside of me. Then one evening at twenty weeks, I began to feel very uneasy. I was in pain, and it was happening in intervals. I rushed to the hospital only to learn that I was in labor at twenty weeks. They began to treat me immediately with magnesium sulfate to attempt to slow down the premature labor. I cried, asking God to please allow my baby to live. It was a long night, but the next morning, the doctor came into the room to tell me that if I showed up just a few minutes later than I did, I would have lost my baby. From that day on, I spent many days on and off in the high-risk ward at St. Peter's Hospital in New Brunswick, New Jersey. I was immediately put on 100 percent bedrest with only bathroom privileges. Suddenly I was on the sidelines of life, and everything came to a halt. I could no longer cook or clean the house. We got a small refrigerator and put it in the room so I could walk just a few feet to get lunch while I was home alone all day. I had to get progesterone shots. I always recall my sister coming to wash my hair in a bowl and braiding it for me. Looking back at it now, I felt alone. Thankfully, my family did as much as they could during that time.

For the next few weeks, I went through various episodes of pre-term labor. I even wore a special belt around my stomach to try to detect the cramping. While I was married at that time, I still remember feeling like I was on the journey alone. Things were already rocky, and it seemed to be just a matter of time before it all exploded. But at that moment, I knew I had to focus on getting Joshua into the world safely with God's help. It was touch and go most days. Then one day at twenty-seven weeks, the contractions began. Except for this time, no medicine would stop the contractions. My doctor rushed to the hospital, and the Neonatal Intensive Care Unit (NICU) was alerted that there was a premature baby on the way. The physician from the NICU came in to tell me that they had a team of people waiting for my baby, and it was going to be okay. My mother and family were alerted and rushed from New York City to be by my side.

When the labor could no longer be stopped, the physician rushed me into the delivery room. I began crying out to God in my heart, saying "I can't do this! Lord, this does not make sense! I didn't even have a baby shower! Where is my perfect pregnancy?". I began to push at the doctor's direction, and I was tiring fast because of all the activity before being in the delivery room. After numerous tries, I could feel the birthing come forth. There were teams of doctors in the room running around.

I heard a faint cry from my son, and it seemed like the world stopped. The next sound I heard was "Code Blue! Code Blue!". The nurse ran over to me and Joshua's dad with tears in her eyes and said, "Pray for your baby." I knew when the nurse cried; there was trouble. At that moment, I turned away from the table where Joshua's little body laid. I could not bear to watch him lay there, lifeless. The doctor asked for the heartbeat, but there was no heartbeat. No one could answer. I began to cry, and my mother and husband were by my side, crying as well. It was all happening so fast, but it felt like time was standing still. On my hospital bed, I whispered through my tears, "God, I need you."

Just then, I heard the doctors call out – "Call for the Priest!". That was the signal that death had entered the room. My crying became more frantic, and then one doctor's direction changed the entire story. She yelled out, "One More Epi! Let's try one more Epi!". The doctors followed her lead, and seconds later, I heard a cry from my little two-pound baby. It was faint but strong at the same time. The machines began to beep, signaling Joshua's heart rate returned. And everyone started running around the room, preparing the incubator to transport Joshua to the NICU.

The priest came running in and was astonished at the scene before him. I heard him declare in a loud voice, "I was coming to read the last rites, but now I'm here to bless this baby! He read Psalms 23, and all those who knew it by heart repeated along with the priest. The doctors picked up Joshua, and as they put him in the incubator, they brought him over to me to kiss him on his tiny cheek. I could not believe he was here!

As the doctors wheeled him away in the incubator, his father ran behind them in desperation, wanting to know his baby boy would make it. My mother and I were left in the room, and I never cried like I did that day. You could hear us through the entire corridor. My mother comforted me in a way that only a mother could comfort a child. In those moments, I could feel God's assurance that I had just experienced my moment with God. Joshua was sent to the NICU and had to have chest tubes inserted, and there were wires coming from everywhere. He weighed in at 2 pounds, 7 ounces. He was the littlest person I ever saw. His father could hold him in the palm of his hand. For sixty days, I traveled to Saint Peter's Hospital in New Brunswick, New Jersey, to carry him through this journey. We had some setbacks, but through it all, I walked out of the hospital on day sixty with my little miracle. Thankfully, the hyperthyroidism resolved after I had Joshua, and life seemed to be finding some sense of normal.

My days for the next few years were filled with doctor's visits to track his development and follow up on his heart and breathing conditions. I gave my entire focus to ensuring he received the best care possible. He went through surgeries, and it was all very taxing for him and our family with two additional near-death experiences. Yet, God remained faithful to bring us through every season. The name Joshua means "God is Salvation." We chose Joshua's name in the early weeks of my pregnancy, not realizing how much his name would say to him. Despite such a rough beginning, Joshua grew up with no developmental deficiencies and is my child who loves attention and always has some humor up his sleeve.

The words "One More Epi" were a defining moment for us in the delivery room. Over time I learned how important that decision was from a clinical standpoint. Epi refers to epinephrine, which is also known as adrenaline. Adrenaline is a hormone that is typically produced by the adrenal glands. Epinephrine is used medically to treat many conditions, including cardiac arrest. Joshua's body was not ready for the early delivery, and he needed some extra support to breathe. It appeared that all hope was lost, but the doctor's faith called for one more try. "One More Epi" was a game-changer for me and still is.

When I picture that day in the delivery room, I can still hear that day thirteen years later. I can even see all the activity. Most of all, I can again re-live the miracle of what happened to us that day. Miracles happen, but it is just a matter of us not missing the miracles that we are graced to come across in our own lives – small or large.

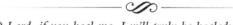

O Lord, if you heal me, I will truly be healed; If you save me, I will be truly saved. My praises are for you alone.
—Jeremiah 17:14

From the day that I stood at the altar in prayer for my womb to be opened until this very day, it has been a faith walk with my oldest son Joshua. There have been many nights in which I laid before God in prayer, asking for strength and direction. I had to learn medical terminology to be able to communicate with his various specialist effectively. By the time Joshua was three years old, he was on a Continuous Pressure Airway Pressure (CPAP) Machine due to enlarged tonsils and adenoids.

Before obtaining the machine, we attempted to remove the tonsils and adenoids with hopes it would relieve his condition. The surgery went well, but Joshua appeared to be in distress just a few hours after surgery. Liquid began to flood his lungs, and he had to be rushed into Intensive Care and placed on a ventilator. For fourteen days, Joshua remained on the ventilator. His small three-year-old body seemed so helpless. I stayed by his side for fourteen days straight–barely leaving for showers. It was a replay of his first sixty days of life in the NICU. I don't recall talking to anyone much during that time. I am not even sure what I did for all that time while I sat there. I remember our families coming to visit. It all felt like a blur.

Through God's grace, Joshua came off the ventilator two weeks later. I expected him to wake up and be talkative and bouncing around the room as he had done prior. But instead, he sat there and stared at me as if he wasn't sure who I was. I reassured him it was Mommy, and his Dad did as well. We took him home a few days later, and life did not immediately snap back to normal. For weeks, Joshua woke up in the middle of the night, screaming from nightmares! We would hold him and console him back to sleep. His doctor assured us that it was a side effect of all the drugs and time he was on the ventilator, and he would come around soon. I held on to this hope and continued to labor with Joshua each night, and eventually, one night, he slept straight through the night. It was my first night of resting as well after weeks of waking up all night.

Joshua's journey started with a dose of adrenaline, and I believe it symbolized the energy and boost that we would need for the ride.

From heart surgeries to ear tubes, Joshua has had to withstand a tremendous amount at his young age. Every time he endured pain; my heart would break. I would continually present Joshua back to God as his gift on loan to me. I would ask God to help me take the best care of him that I could do. I dedicated my energy and focused on the journey.

I want to encourage the parent who may have experienced dealing with a child who was born prematurely and or experienced illness. No matter what the situation is, I must identify the fact that first, it is heart-wrenching. Secondly, it can be taxing emotionally and physically. You may spend more time diagnosing and treating, rather than just simply enjoying your child. There were periods where I remembered a doctor's visit notes more than I remembered a milestone that Joshua had that week. His conditions and care needed threatened to overshadow the pure joy of just growing with my child.

I recall buying Joshua a Bumbo as he got a little older and started sitting up. The Bumbo was a small rubber chair that could support his lower back and provide cushioning for his bottom and legs as he stood up. I was sitting in the living room doing something busily, and a commercial came on the television. This commercial had a catchy beat to it. I heard Joshua make a little sound, and I looked over, and he was rocking to the beat! I was amazed that he was on the exact timing with the rhythm, and it drove me into fits of smiling and laughing. Joshua noticed that this made me happy and continued to do it. It was our moment, and I knew that day he would like music. He started to dance at an early age and has begun to learn the drums. Despite all going on at that time, I'm grateful that I could capture those moments in my heart and mind.

It's no mistake that Joshua's defining moment in life began with the words "One More Epi!" We have needed those words more than once. It's been the adrenaline of faith and prayer that has continued to push us through. It was the adrenaline of love that allowed us to continue to fight for Joshua – even when he couldn't fight for himself. As a toddler, he would stand out among his peers because he needed a machine to help him breathe at naptime. I always sought to make him feel secure in being different. I had to feel unashamed so that he could feel that way as well. How we perceive our life is how it will appear to us. It would take an entire book to list and describe all the answered prayers since Joshua arrived. So many have prayed for Joshua – some that knew him personally and others who didn't.

Our journey was not private. I had to be transparent in my struggles so that others could help hold up my arms. There is a story in the Bible where Moses goes out to war with the Amalekites, and as the Israelites fight, he holds up the stick that God told him to carry (Exodus 17: 8 – 13). Yet something powerful happens – each time Moses drops the stick because his arms grew tired, the Israelites would start to lose the battle. But when he raised the stick again, they would begin to win. When Moses became weary, Aaron and Hur brought a stone to sit on, and they held up his arms until the sun went down so the battle could be won. This biblical account has always reminded me that there are some battles and journeys that we can't walk through alone. There are periods where we need someone to hold up our arms.

I've needed others to hold up my arms as I grew tired in caring for my premature baby. I needed some extra prayers to go along with mines. I needed someone to verbalize words when my words were all lost to tears. The moral of the story is that the adrenaline we need for our life journeys does not always come from within. At times, we need one more dose of hope and faith to be injected into our spiritual veins to give us what we need to keep going forward.

2

God Did it Again

*Sometimes we place limits on what can happen in
our lives when God has even more in store.*

Although my life was not going as great as it needed to, I continued
to press forward in my relationship. I had a baby boy that was born
prematurely and needed my strength. I needed the support of my
spouse and tried to hang on for dear life. As soon as Joshua was
strong enough, I took a trip south to bring him to meet my maternal
grandmother and family in Alabama. I was excited to go back to
my grandmother's church with the fruit of my womb! I remember
putting a little outfit on Joshua and brushing his hair to get him all
ready.

This time I took the trip alone south, and when the pastor called
me up to greet the church, I began to tell the story of Joshua's miracle
conception and how God saved him in the delivery room and had
been faithful to us! The church was ecstatic and rejoiced with me as
I shared my testimony. When the pastor asked to pray for me again,
I somehow knew I was about to be set up for a second time around!
The words he prayed have stuck with me since that very day over
eleven years ago. I recall him saying, "Now Lord, this child Joshua
you have given her is not hers, he is Yours. Now give her a child she
can call her own." And his wife proceeded to pray for me once again.

When I left the church that afternoon, I went on about life.

Based on my history, I figured if it took me seven years to get pregnant the first time, then I had at least seven years to wait for the next. Little did I know! On that upcoming Mother's Day, I went to the pharmacy and brought a Sunday paper and pregnancy test. Once again, I missed my menstrual cycle, but it was not abnormal since I suffered from irregular periods. I decided to test anyway as I had done for many years before Joshua. Much to my surprise, the test was positive! I couldn't believe it. I sat on the floor of the bathroom in both shock and awe.

Because of my first experience with Joshua, my doctors treated me as a high risk immediately. I was placed on progesterone injections and received a cerclage within the first ten weeks. The cerclage was meant to keep the cervix closed and secure with hopes of preventing pre-term labor. This time I did not get sick at all. I felt normal, aside from being on bed rest as early as ten weeks. I spent my days going from the couch to the bed. Often, I sat on a chair in the kitchen to cook me a meal. Once again, I still remember feeling alone during those times when I think back. During my pregnancy, things were getting even harder in my marriage.

I recall one night being home alone, and I opened my Bible. The pages fell right to the book of Jeremiah, Chapter 1. And these words seemed to come alive right off the page.

I knew you before I formed you in your mother's womb. Before you were born, I set you apart and appointed you as my spokesman to the world.
—Jeremiah 1:5

That was over eleven years ago, and the tears well up even now as I write these words. I recall being on the couch, and I looked down at my small growing belly and said, "I will lay here on this couch as long as I need to get you here safely. Your name will be Jeremiah." I believe his dad had other names in line for him, but that night, no one in the world could convince me to name my baby anything else

You are viewing a preview of this image. To view the full image, please upgrade.

except Jeremiah! I waited there on the couch and bed for twenty weeks until his arrival could not be held back any longer.

The day my water broke was a long day indeed. My oldest son had severe sleep apnea and needed to have surgery at Children's Hospital of Philadelphia. I was thirty weeks at the time and was excited to have made it this far in my pregnancy. It was three weeks longer than I carried Josh, and I knew every single day counted in the womb. I could not bear to have Joshua go through surgery without me there, although it was outpatient. I decided that I needed to get out and try to make it to be there for my baby. The day was long as we waited, and after surgery, my mother offered for Joshua and me to come to her house in New York so she could help me with Joshua after his surgery. Needing the help, we took the ride from Philadelphia back to New York.

We finally settled in, and I went to go lay down. Suddenly I felt water running down my legs, and I was afraid even to see what it was. I called my mom into the room, and with tears in my eyes, I said, "Mom, I think my water just broke." She inspected my wet clothing, looked at me, and said, "Oh No, Nikki, I'm so sorry." I immediately got the phone to call my doctor's emergency line to tell them I was thirty weeks, and it looked like my baby was on the way. My doctors were in New Jersey, so I was at least one hour away. My doctor instructed me to put a towel under me and try to make it there. I had no contractions at the time, so we had a little time to get to the hospital. I've never seen my mom drive that fast in my life! She made it to New Jersey in less than forty-five minutes and even had a police escort!

I remember turning around and seeing my little Joshua in the backseat, and I had this sinking feeling that this would be my life. That it would be these two babies and me, but I could not process it at that time. I called Joshua's dad and my sisters so they could all meet me at the hospital. The doctors rushed me in to remove the cerclage so they could monitor my cervix. I still did not have contractions, and by way of a miracle, I was able to carry Jeremiah for five more days there in the hospital. Each day they checked the fluids to make sure he was still safe. On the fifth day, the contractions began, and we knew it was time to move forward.

I initially tried to do vaginal delivery as I had done with Joshua. I pushed and pushed, but Jeremiah was not coming forth. Each time I tried to push him out, his heart rate would drop on the monitors. The doctors made a quick decision to send me to the operating room for C-section surgery. They pushed me quickly down the hallways to get to the operation because Jeremiah's heart rate was still dropping. I heard the doctors say, "We have to go ahead and get him out, or he won't make it." The anesthesiologist was still attempting to give me anesthesia, but suddenly, I could feel the incision being made to start the C-section. I started screaming, "I feel it; I feel the cutting!" The nurse rubbed my face and told me to hold on for one moment, and soon I would not feel it anymore. She said, "We need to get the baby out now."

I recall screaming from pain, and then suddenly, it all went black. When I woke up, it was three hours later. I had been in surgery for hours after due to complications. My first words were "Where is my baby?" – slurred and barely able to speak. They assured me he was alive and well and in the Neonatal Intensive Care Unit (NICU). From there, I fell asleep again to recover from all that happened. That night I went down to the NICU to see my newest baby boy under blue lights in his incubator. He was 3 pounds, 16 ounces, and he was breathing on his own. I'll never forget the moment I reached in to touch his little hands. Right then, I knew that God had given me another miracle.

When I sit and think about this journey, it humbles me tremendously. Jeremiah was born with hemorrhaging on the brain. The neurologist sat with me to talk about all the potential outcomes – cerebral palsy, shunts for the brain, limited mobility, or verbal difficulties. The list was endless. Truly my faith was being tested. I now had a 21- month old toddler with numerous conditions that I had to continue to follow up on and now a newborn with brain trauma - something I could not see or measure but could affect life for my child long-term. Jeremiah was such a pleasant baby. He rarely cried, and he could be laid down and would be content all by himself. Maybe he remembered being there with me on the couch all those evenings when we were alone. Each day I would stretch his legs and rub his head declaring healing over him.

We had regular check-ins with the neurologist to keep track of his progress. Many of the symptoms would not possibly show up until he was a little older, so it was a process of waiting. But while I was waiting – I was praying! Jeremiah had to have a follow-up CT Scan within the first year to check in on how he was doing. The day we met with the doctor to go over the results, I was nervous but felt strongly about God working a miracle for Jeremiah, so I walked in that faith. That day the doctor shared the great news with me – the blood in Jeremiah's brain receded on its' own and was absorbed by the body. He was not going to need a shunt and should walk as normal! It took all I had in me not to jump up and shout in that hospital room!

I continued to exercise Jeremiah's legs, and at fourteen months, my baby boy took his first steps. What a glorious day that was. Jeremiah is now eleven- years old and loves to play basketball. I took a picture of him recently jumping up to shoot the ball, and I could only praise God for his ability to do that. It was indeed God's doing!! And he is smart as a whip bringing home straight A's, and he is the wittiest little guy you would want to meet. Most of all, he never goes to bed without giving me hugs at night. He loves affection and is very thoughtful.

The birth of Jeremiah was Part 2 of my beginnings. Five months into Jeremiah's birth, I was officially separated and on my own. I lived in New Jersey on my own for a few months and decided to move back to New York to live with my mother during this delicate season of my life. My experiences over the next ten years became my chronicles: the good, the bad, and the ugly. But through it all, I knew this beginning was not the end. It was only the start of a path I had to take. Only God knows and understands all our steps. We can sit back and rationalize that there were things we could do differently all day long. But ultimately, I learned to embrace where I was so I wouldn't miss my blessing!

In Jeremiah's early years, I had to learn how to adjust my parenting as I now had a double blessing! Alongside being a single parent, I had the delicate balance of nurturing two premature babies. In the NICU, they gave me the title of "Frequent Flyer." This title was the way moms who had more than one preemie were acknowledged. When a nurse initially said that to me, I felt a tinge of guilt for being there more than once. I wanted to have a full, healthy pregnancy and saw my place in the NICU as a downfall to that desire. But then I caught the revelation that frequent flyers are unique on airlines. It means they have been there, and they know the ropes. And so it was with my NICU mom status! I knew my way around, and I was ultimately able to help others. During Jeremiah's stay, I elevated in my knowledge and my confidence that God would do it again. The "it" for me in this part of my story was not just the baby, but it was also the deliverance of bringing us through the difficult moment.

If I had to close this chapter with any words of encouragement, I would have to say that God can do anything we need. We can walk through the seasons we need to walk through. I gained and lost at the same time, yet it was clear that I was gaining strength. Enjoy the moment you are in right now. Please write down what makes you laugh so you can recall it later in life with your children. Expect the strength you need to walk the journey!

3

Why Your Story is Important

*Stories are not just words written on the
pages of a book. Stories are the journey of the
heart. Some of which are never written.*

I started this book off by telling you my story. Not with a heavy focus on how I became single, but how I became a mother. As single parents, it is easy to focus on your status of "single" and miss the word right behind it, which is even more important – "parent". Single is defined as a person rather than a group. A parent is defined as a father or mother. Somewhere down the line, those two terms were combined to mean a person bringing up a child or children without a partner.

On top of that, there was a stigma attached to the status that indicated a potential lack. Regardless of the story of how things turned out with your partner or if a partner was involved at all, your role as a parent is the most dominant factor in all of this. You can parent and raise healthy and whole children. That is why your story is essential.

I can recall throughout the years meeting people, and they would say, "So what's your story?" I would always start with my youth, my failed marriage, and then my children. It was as if my story had to have this chronology in front of it to be meaningful. What if my story simply started like this: "I am the mom of two amazing young men I have had the pleasure of raising. Along with being a mom, I am a career woman, and I love and enjoy my life!" What a different narrative this is than the original story I was used to telling.

A story is considered an account of past events or in the evolution of something. The narrative you speak will determine your outlook.

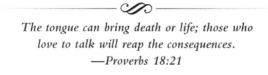

*The tongue can bring death or life; those who
love to talk will reap the consequences.*
—Proverbs 18:21

Have you ever felt a tinge of shame as you told your story about your life and being a single parent? It's easy to feel like there was some failure that caused this to be the outcome. I became a single mom when my youngest son was five months old. Initially, it seemed like it would be a cakewalk but not too much longer I realized that being a single mom with two young children was going to be one of the most challenging yet rewarding journeys in my life. I had this stigma attached to my story and even felt ashamed. My mother was a single parent, and I felt like I inherited this status by some generational downfall. Honestly, my self-esteem was damaged. I hoped people would accept me and even carried that weight on my shoulder when I tried to date. I had been through a tremendous journey and knew my children were a gift – yet why did I still struggle with me?

The struggle existed because I attached my relationship reality to my role as a parent. I made my story all-inclusive, and it is not. I am single, and that is because I am divorced. And I am divorced because my marriage struggled, and we mutually decided to end it. And we agreed to end it because it seemed like the right and sane thing to do at that time. And I could go on and on. But do you see the pattern here? As I explained my single status, I did not mention my children. It's because they are not the reason or the story for why I am single.

Now on the other end, I am a parent. And the reason I am a parent is that I have children. I have children because I desired children, and by a miracle, I was able to give birth to them. And this miracle of their birth is the greatest blessing I can ever experience. And I am now free from the stigma that I attached to being single and parenting because I realized that one low moment does not define my blessing to be a parent here on this earth. And freedom comes when we look at our situations through the lens of God, not the lens of what the world defines as success. Statistics can speak to numbers and figures, but they cannot always explain the concepts of blessings. The statistical aspect of my situation may be clear for the world to see, but the benefit I feel as a parent is hidden in my heart. And then I can operate from that place of love in my heart as I raise my sons because I understand the blessing in it.

I am writing this book to share my story, and I hope that at least one person will be able to grasp this concept of re-writing and re-defining their story. When "re" is placed in front of a word, it typically means "again" or "back." There are some stories that you need to write again. Not that you need to live it again – but to write them again so that the re-write is at the forefront of how you operate with it. Whenever anything is written, any updates to it are revisions. Revisions are allowable in almost any type of work. The sooner you revise – the better. If I am publishing this book, it is way more cost-effective for me to make revisions in the publishing phase. And even then, there are phases of publishing where revisions become more costly. Once the book hits the shelves, it becomes harder to pull it back and re-distribute with changes.

The sooner, the better and the time to re-vise your story is now. The dash in-between is not a grammatical mistake. I want to draw your attention to the second half of the word – vise. A vise is a mechanical device used to hold an object firmly in place while work is done on it. Vises typically have two parallel jaws, threaded in by a screw and lever. You can find vises in many places such as a woodworker's bench, metalworker bench, etc. Regardless of the shape or use, the primary purpose is to hold something in place to allow work.

Understanding this word became an "Aha" moment for me because, to re-define my story, some elements had to hold it in place so I could work on it. I can say my faith has kept it in place, allowing me to work on it. My dreams and aspirations to be more than a statistic has kept my life in place to enable me to work on it. My desire to bypass the pain and see the bright future ahead has worked as a vise in my life to allow me to work on it. My love for my two miracle boys has been a significant vise in my life that has held my life in place to make the revisions I needed to make at the right timing. What has been the vise in your life? What has kept things in place so you can work on you and your journey?

That is what the scriptures mean when they say, "No eye has seen, no ear has heard, and no mind has imagined what God has prepared for those who love him."
—1 Corinthians 2:9

I think about re-defining my story, there is another part of the word re-vision that sticks out. The word "vision" is the ability to see but also references the manifestation of something that is not always material. Vision involves being able to imagine and dream of what can lie ahead. You cannot re-write your story without a strong sense of vision. There must be something that may not be visible now, but that your heart has been able to imagine ahead. No matter how you became a single parent, there is no indication that you lost vision and promise. Remember, "single" is a separate word from "parent."

Your story is remarkable, and you should take account of how you have been telling it. There was a time in my life that all I talked about was how I got to the place of being single and parenting. That story defined me. I wondered if I could climb the corporate ladder with my story. Every step I took up the ladder, I looked back at my story as if it were something I needed to pull up with me, rather than seeing it as a part of me. Instead, I began embracing the success story of still being able to work hard and achieve more for my boys and me. Your account is just as relevant now as it will ever be. Re-write and re-tell your story if you need to.

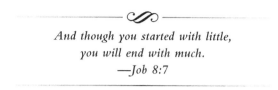

And though you started with little,
you will end with much.
—Job 8:7

My heart's desire for this book is to breed a movement and declaration of the blessing in the lives of those who parent alone. This message is essential and needs to be heard. I even want to wear a T-shirt with it! As I journeyed through my life as a single parent, I did not always see the blessing in it because I had a different idea in mind for how my life would turn out. But the true message is that my children are my blessing – regardless of what I have experienced! My strength to live and move forward has come through the God-given grace to raise my sons. And if we don't embrace that message early in the journey, we will lose precious time in frustration, anxiety, and regret. I dare to say the "R" word – regret. It's the word that we don't want to speak to anyone but secretly robs us of our peace. I don't want to write comfortably – I want to acknowledge the profound truth. The reality is there were times of asking questions of myself like "What signs did I miss?" and "This is not fair to my sons." These types of statements clog the heart from being able to embrace the beauty of life itself.

In the scripture above, Job is in a place of a complete breakdown. He had lost everything from his family to his possessions. Yet he receives this message from his friend, that although he has a little now, he will end with much more. In the concept of our lives, this does not always refer to financial gain. Although I started out on my parenting journey with a little joy, I am yet gaining much joy. I may have started my journey with a little experience, but I am progressing in my quest to a place of many experiences. I started with a little peace and gained much peace throughout the years. There is an ability to increase despite where you are.

Your story is all that you have to represent to the world. I am calling forth those who are willing to re-write and re-tell their stories so they can be the change they want to see in their lives. I was riding in my car one evening, and I was thinking about something going on in my life. At that moment, a song came on the radio called "Change Me" by Gospel Artist, Tamela Mann. The song is a heart cry for God to change us. Suddenly, I began to say, "God, my situation may not change, but change me!" I said that about three times, and then the floodgates of tears broke. I had tapped into a new place within, and the tears were a sign of release. My eyes were flooded on the way home as I acknowledged that I didn't have to wait for my situation to change – I could start with myself. And this is the transformation that I seek to share in this work. That when we begin to look at the blessings in our life instead of the circumstances – there is a transformation that starts from the inside out. And it will be evident and contagious to those around us. Our story is where it begins!

4

Organize, Organize, and Trust

*The act of organizing does not promise there will
never be any chaos. Rather, organizing provides
preparation that leads to sanity amid any chaos.*

Imagine a five-month-old and a two-year-old in a gray double stroller with two diaper bags and all of this getting on a New York Subway at 6 a.m. in the Bronx with hopes of making it to a job at 8 a.m. in New Jersey via mass transit. Couple with daycare drop off at the office (that cost $200 a week per child, by the way) and running to an elevator to make it upstairs in a corporate office and then skillfully using elevator time to shake off all the anxiety and stress of the past two hours to start a day as a leader. You utilize lunch breaks to see the new five-month-old baby and feed him baby food to make a connection with him. Then, hiding and ducking while you pass the preschool class, so your two-year-old will not have a full meltdown because he sees you and you are not taking him home yet!

On lunch, you go to the Mother's room to pump breastmilk so your baby can at least get one bottle. Of course, because of all the stress, you are not producing as much milk as you should! By 4:30 p.m., after solving problems all day, you get off work and jump right back on the train. Get home by 7:00 p.m. that evening and race to make a meal for you and the babies. Babies to bed by 8:30 p.m., but your bedtime extends to 11 p.m. so you can prepare everything to do the same show all over again tomorrow. The alarm goes off at 4:30 a.m. the next morning, and the curtains pull back for the show to begin anew!

I know this sounds like something out of a reality TV show! Comical, to say the least. This show was my life every day during the first two years of single motherhood. I moved back to the Bronx, New York, to live with my mom so I could have a support system. It was not a tough decision because my mom is my best friend, and I knew we would be fine living together. But the harsh reality was I was moving from one state to the next, and it was going to require me to keep it all afloat with a whole lot more to navigate. I had always been a somewhat organized person, but I learned how much organizing meant during this season.

One of the things I had to learn early on was to write reminders down. The brain moves quickly, and when raising children, constant insertions (I will not call it interruptions) require your attention. It's easy to lose track of what you need to do daily. I found that walking around with a piece of paper or notepad helped me to jot down those things that pop into my head at a meeting or while taking care of the kids. This practice promoted my wellbeing because I was able to free up that space in my mind for something else. And there was always something else waiting right behind it to jump in line! Now with smartphones, it is easy to add notes to your phone.

Another strategy I found was organizing the children's clothes for the week ahead. If I was having a good week, my clothes for the work week might be set aside a week ahead too. I had bins for each day of the week, and I threw (literally) clothes into a container so I could pull them out in the mornings. I also packed the diaper bags ahead of time. Although my boys are older now, I still use some of these strategies, such as laundry baskets. When they were toddlers, I never thought I would see the day when they would do laundry. Thank God for growth!

For most of my years as a single parent, I lived in places that did not have washer and dryers right in my apartment, so my Saturday mornings were filled with early trips to the laundromat with my boys. I had three different apartments over five years in Newark, New Jersey. Very few even had washer and dryer hookups. My sons were too young to help me do the laundry and carry the bags, so I gained a lot of muscle during those years from carrying loads of bags. I never forget having an apartment on the third floor of a private house. Can you imagine dragging those bags up almost six long flights of stairs? I had to stay organized in virtually every intricate area of my life. From timing how long it took me to get everything loaded, to getting back upstairs to the children before they noticed I ran outside.

You may be saying, "Nikki, that's all easier said than done." But what I will say is that "organization" does not equal "perfection." "Organization" equals "efficiency" and efficiency means to achieve maximum productivity with minimum wasted effort and expense. Let that sink in for a minute! I am sure you can relate to a whole lot of wasted effort and cost. And you were feeling like you had not achieved much after racing against a clock all day long. That's not organization – that is chaos. I am super familiar with that. Efficiency means that you will get things done, but still have some energy left on reserve for another day. Efficiency means you pull out less of your hair, and then your hair grows! Efficiency means you get to go to bed at night too. And sleep doesn't become something that you feel is just for the privileged. Efficiency means you learn to say No and Yes, at the same time. Say No to allowing your circumstances to drive your level of control and Yes to allowing yourself to "be" despite your circumstances.

Another major area to focus on is the organization of your schedule. Some days I had to organize down to the minute to help with knowing where to be and when. It was easy to organize my schedule in the early years because the kids were in daycare and preschool with no extra-curricular activities. My primary program was my work schedule, and I limited my extra-curricular activities while they were school. I attended church services weekly, and that was most of my life excitement in the younger years. My boys were not the kids who got to church and sat down in one spot. They wanted to roam and fight, and I would feel like a failure of a mom for being unable to control them completely.

I can recall going to church one Sunday, and my oldest son, who was a toddler at the time, acted out so badly that I packed them up and left the church before it was over. I remember crying the whole way home and saying. "God, I can't even go to church!" I was so frustrated with my life and the way it was going. I wanted to give the appearance that I had this single mom thing altogether. And I saw my son acting out as someone holding up a sign over my head that said I did not have it altogether! Yet, it was such a blessing that I had pressed my way there despite all it took to get organized on a Sunday morning. But I could not celebrate the win of organizing because I was too focused on my son's behavior as a sign of failure. Years later, my sons are attentive to church services and gives me no heartache to get ready to go.

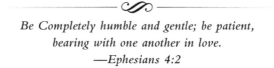

Be Completely humble and gentle; be patient,
bearing with one another in love.
—Ephesians 4:2

Patience has been my greatest lesson in all seasons of this journey. I had to learn how to be patient with my children. The strain of parenting and leading a home can be extremely taxing and it can strip away your ability to parent with patience. But my sons have taught me daily, how much patience affords us. I bear with them in love as they bear with me in love.

Both of my children were born before their baby showers. Since Joshua was so premature, I could not have a baby shower there in the beginning because he stayed in the NICU for two months. His 1-year-old birthday party was more like a baby shower. Jeremiah only remained in the NICU for one month, so I was able to have a baby shower in my mother's backyard not long after he was born. It was a baby shower barbeque! My son's grandmother (may her soul rest in peace) gave me the best gift of the day, which was a shiny double stroller equipped with a toddler style seat and the baby bed in the front. It also had a carriage underneath and two spots for a bottle and a sippy cup. I remember Mom Kelly saying to me, "You are going to need this." She was so right. That double stroller became my saving grace for years to come.

What's so important about the double stroller? Its obvious use is to give parents the ability to transport. The stroller has a double meaning – one meaning is a chair on wheels for a child. The other meaning is someone taking a stroll or a leisurely walk. I did a lot of embracing that first definition, but I did not do a lot of the second. The stroller was meant to lighten my load and allow me to take a walk through that season and my journey. I understand now why Mom Kelly said I would need it. There were apparent reasons I needed it, but it was also going to be one of the staples of my journey. There is not much I did not do in that gray double stroller. And I can't quite recall the day I put it aside.

No matter what stage of the journey you are in, don't forget to stroll. Go for a walk in the park and be conscious of your stroll and the sounds around you. Now that my sons are older, it requires just as much organization as I balance health outcomes, career, sports, education, and everything else that comes my way. It is always super important that I am not still in a place of burden but that I learn how to take a stroll and take it all in stride.

Staying organized helps give you some control and take away some of the anxiety that you may be feeling. Even if you do not know where to start - start small. Find one area that you know makes you "flip the script" daily and try to come up with a plan to do it differently. For me, it is sometimes the after-work burn where my patience is low and not much left for the kids, so I am always trying to find ways to make the evening less hectic. Whether it is preparing meals ahead or just doing my chores before work in the morning, I always look for those strategies that help me. I discovered the beauty of the crockpot a few years back, and that has become a trusty friend as well that I use to help me get me through a trying week.

I have read tons of books on organization, and there are

many resources out there to help you organize. I have learned that organization should not just be limited to my home chores, children's activities, and schools. But there is an internal organization that I needed to have in place as well. How I organize my thoughts and perception are crucial to how I view my world, my children, and the world around me. Daily I must tune in to my thoughts to ensure I keep positive ones ahead of doubt and fear. When we consciously focus on the organization of our thoughts, it creates space for transparent decision-making each day.

Another area that I learned had to remain organized in my life as a single parent is my finances. Many years ago, I had trouble keeping up with payments and due dates amid all I was doing. And of course, I kept spending because it was necessary to meet the needs of my home. This course of living became a recipe for disaster financially, and I had to grab hold of it. I started to create a spreadsheet of my bills month over month and record due dates and payments. I still use this method to this day, and I anticipate remaining on that path. It is a simple way for me to stay organized. Everyone may have a technique – it does not matter how you do it. Find what works for you.

While organizing the home, family life, and finances, we must also remember to plan our future. I live with the daunting truth that my children may outlive me. And I must have a plan around how they will be taken care of. I know their father will take care of them if he is living, but I have my obligation as their primary custodial parent for their whole life. Whether through living wills, insurance policies, or savings account – I have begun to focus on the future for them. One of my sons is just five years from college, which raises a whole other topic of funding college for two boys. I have already encouraged them to look towards scholarships thru academics and sports so we can have options. I'm excited when I think about their lives ahead. I know they will depend on me to support them financially in those exciting times of their lives. I realize the choices and decisions I make over the next five years will impact them as well.

This chapter is one that I write out of awareness, not perfection. Daily I seek to find better ways to organize my life. But organization must begin with prioritization. And my priority is my faith and relationship with God. I realize that there is someone bigger than me that has allowed me to stay this course. If I can keep my faith at the forefront, and my family next in line, all else will continue to fall in place.

Seek the Kingdom of God above all else, and live righteously, and he will give you everything you need.
—Matthew 6:33

5

4 a.m. Study Sessions

Dreams are not categorized according to age and privileges afforded in life. Dreams are available to anyone who will close their eyes and envision something new.

Merriam Webster defines dreams as a cherished aspiration, ambition, or ideal. I start with this definition to add context to this chapter because it is vital to settle what a dream is. I have seen countless single mothers who delay their dreams and aspirations to manage their life calling to parent their children. My hopes of gaining a higher education were delayed before I even had children. I kept missing the timeframe of opportunity through my life distractions and lack of focus on the goal. However, when my children were toddlers, I finally decided to pursue my dream of an undergraduate degree. I enrolled in a school that offered a mix of traditional and online classes. I did not have someone in the home to commit to taking care of my children in the evenings, so I knew I could not go the traditional route. Online education has become very accessible today.

Initially, I came home each day and worked through the evening grind. Then at 8:30 p.m., I would attempt to sit down with my books, and within minutes, my eyes were closing. After a long day at work, it did not seem easy even to think. One evening I decided to go to bed on time and wake up at 4 a.m. It was a shot in the dark, but

I hoped it would work. Miraculously I was able to get two complete hours of study before my children even woke up. It was tough at first to get up at that time, but I soon started to see the benefits of waking up early for my routine. I felt less stressed and impatient in the evening with the children, which was beneficial to them and me.

The word "dream" in the noun sense refers to the thoughts and images that you may experience in your sleep, cherished ambition, or ideal. I had to add this part of my reflections because I was always an avid reader and learner. I did well in my younger years of schooling when I was focused. I traditionally could achieve high grades, and writing was something that flowed from me like water. My mother always reminds me of my English teacher in elementary school, Mrs. Robinson. She met my mother and me on the school sidewalk one day and began to tell my mother how important writing would be in my life. That day is still so vivid in my mind. I can remember it being a sunny day, but trees shaded the area where we stood. I remember the sound of the cars honking for the kids as parents pulled up. I do not quite remember why my mother was standing on the sidewalk instead of sitting inside her car that day. Mrs. Robinson looked down at me and said, "Nicole, you have a gift. Don't stop writing." I felt a spark in her words that day, and I knew I wanted to pursue my education.

When I graduated high school, I originally applied to colleges out of state. The cost that my mother would have to take on to allow me to go was not feasible. I decided to do college locally. Through a series of events before I knew it, I was married and, in the workforce, (that is a whole separate book that I will write someday). My jobs became the primary focus, and the pursuit of college was secondary. But I never let go of that innate desire to pursue my education. Dreams are not always fulfilled in the way that we hope them to be. But the key is never to lose sight and let go of your cherished ambition.

Fast forward to me being a single mom and still not finished with my undergraduate degree. I made a firm decision to put my foot down and plant into the pursuit of my education. For two years, I woke up at 4 a.m. every morning during college classes. I remember sitting at the table of my apartment in Newark, New Jersey, with the books, computer, and printer. I would glance over at my babies. They have always been my inspiration. No one at work knew I was back in school at that time. I think I subconsciously kept it under wraps so that I wouldn't have to explain to anyone if I failed. I wanted to be accountable to myself that I was going to pursue this. And now I had a strong reason to get it done – I was a single mom with two little ones depending on me. My children were too small to remember those days. They knew their breakfast was ready each morning as I woke them up to rise at 6 a.m. each day.

About two weeks before graduation, my youngest son started experiencing a dermatological issue on his legs that caused him to have extreme itching on his legs almost day and night. I took him to numerous doctors to diagnose the problem. We changed detergents, skin lotions, and body washes in the effort to calm the problem. One doctor diagnosed it as viral, so we could not detect the rashes on the skin. He gave him some anti-itch oral medication and advised us that we would need to wait out the process as his body fought it off. I spent many days and nights rubbing his little legs to help calm the sensation of itching. He was miserable!

As graduation approached, I continued to plan for my family to go down to Trenton, New Jersey, to be a part of my big day. All those 4 a.m. sessions were getting ready to materialize with a walk across the stage for my Bachelor of Science in Business Administration degree. My son was still not well, so I arranged with his father to keep him during the graduation ceremonies, and I would pick him up later when I returned. That morning as I pulled out my cap and gown, I looked over and saw my baby rubbing his legs feverishly. I knew right then that I wouldn't be able to leave him and go to graduation. My heart just wouldn't let me. I called my family to tell everyone to halt their plans to travel from New York. I was staying at home with Jeremiah.

I do not think anyone tried too hard to talk me out of it because they knew what my boys meant to me. My one cousin and his wife from New York decided to still come to New Jersey to see me for my big day. I never forget picking them up at the train station, and they were dressed for graduation. They told me to get my cap and gown, and we were going to dinner to celebrate. We went to T.G.I. Fridays and I ordered a nice steak dinner. All the while, I had Jeremiah laying across my lap. I rubbed his legs during my graduation dinner that day while I ate. Funny that while we were there in the restaurant, he got the best sleep I saw him get in a long time. I guess he felt Mommy's peace and wanted to celebrate my day with a peaceful nap. I am always grateful to my cousin and his wife for making that trip on the train to spend time with me. Had they not come; the day may have felt vastly different.

And we know that in all things God works
for the good of those who love him, who have
been called according to his purpose.
—Romans 8:28

My mother, who has always been my biggest cheerleader, said something to me that day that ingrained in my desires. She said, "Nikki, it's ok. This just means you have another graduation ahead of you in life. And that time, you will get to walk." That was back in 2011. Seven years later, I started the journey of earning my master's degree in Business Administration. I relocated to North Carolina to take a new path in my career, and it seemed like the ideal time to make the journey to pursue the next level of my degree. My sons were much older by then and had gained some independence that afforded me some additional time for study. My old trusted 4 a.m. sessions for two years were important again as I pushed through my process of a new job and graduate degree work.

This time I finished my degree sitting through baseball and basketball practices and games. New dynamic – but the same trusted remedies to get through it. I have desired not to sacrifice the moments with the boys to pursue my success. With God's help, I have been able to weave both passions together and maintain balance during it all.

Whenever we press forward on a goal, desire, or dream, there is always a press that occurs in our internal selves that pushes us forward. When you are in pursuit, it may feel as if there are times that you are breaking. But that feeling does not necessarily mean you are breaking in a negative sense. Instead, it is a form of stretching that occurs in your life. We stretch items to expand on the length already there but need some manipulation to pull it forward. When I stretch out a rubber band, I am pulling it out to its potential points, where I can then use it to expand around something else. My 4 a.m. sessions have turned out to be more than just reading. They were my rubber band moments where I stretched out to more significant potential.

No, dear brothers and sisters, I have not achieved
it, but I focus on this one thing; forgetting the
past and looking forward to what lies ahead.
—Philippians 3:13

My chronicle as a single mom has not paused the pursuit of my dreams. As my children get older, I have begun to set sights on their dreams as well. I still have new heights to reach in my faith, personal life, and career. Yes, I have sacrificed much to embrace the journey of being a single mom. But at some point, I realized my role as a mom was not a hindrance. It is my greatest asset. This journey of 4 a.m. sessions caused me to appreciate each accomplishment. And it is a testimony to my children that they can accomplish anything they put their minds towards with hard work, dedication, and focus.

In more ways than one, I felt like I was behind in time in my efforts to pursue greater in my life. There were areas of my life that I thought I could have maximized earlier in life, such as my degree. I had to learn how to combat those thoughts with the assurance that I was right on time. Yes, I may have been able to do it sooner in life, but this was my journey. Because of the press I had to endure to get to this place, I learned to appreciate every effort. Working on my master's degree, stretched my mind and thoughts to new areas in business. I had to take a Financial Accounting class, and it took every effort in my mind, body, and soul to get through that class because math was not my strong subject! My family talks about the fact that I put my desk in my closet, and that was where I worked for six weeks. I would take care of all I had to do for my sons and then go into the closet to get through this class. My sister would call and say, "Where is your mom? Is she is in the closet?" We laugh about it now, but it was serious at the time for me!

I made it through the class, and I remember getting my final grades while I was out with the boys at Chuck E Cheese. I decided to take them to Chuck E Cheese for Joshua's 13th birthday to give him a retro theme of where he loved to go as a toddler! He ran around collecting tickets, just as he had done years ago. When I got the notification that my grade was posted, the boys were playing games, and I was nibbling on a pizza slice. When I saw the grade A on the screen, my heart dropped. I couldn't imagine that I came out with such a high grade! When I looked at the details, it said my average after all assignments were 90.2%, which means I just made it over into the A range.

Before I knew what was happening, my tears began to fall right there with the pizza and phone in hand. The restaurant was full, but for me, it was as if I was having a moment all alone. I put my head down, and all I could say was, "Thank you, thank you," as the tears continued to fall rapidly down my face. I couldn't hold it back if I tried. I put my head up, saw a mom look over at me, and smiled back at her. She nodded at me to acknowledge that somehow, she understood that what I felt at that moment was not grief, rather gratitude. My sons came back to the table and said, "Mommy, are you crying?" I said, "Boys, I made it through the class, and I got an A. I just don't know how I do it. I just don't know how!" They reached over and hugged me and took back off running to play. When we got home, I moved my desk out of the closet to celebrate the completion of a difficult task. It also was a symbol of a shift in the season. Sometimes we must hide away to get through a season in our lives, but the vital part is to know when it is time to come out and celebrate the victory of coming through.

When I graduated last year after pursuing my MBA, my sister took a picture of me with my hands raised in the air. The symbolism of that posture was my raising my hands in thanks to my Father in Heaven, who I know helped me walk the path. At the same time, my raised hands symbolized the letting go of those things in my life that may have held me back. Whether it was regret, shame, procrastination, grief, or lack of confidence, I can release those things when I raise my hands. That is the true outcome of the 4 a.m. sessions – the ability to persevere and stand even when the odds are against you.

6

Rest for the Weary

Rest is our friend who we sometimes promise
we will see soon, when the time is right.

For many years as a single mom, I longed for Saturday morning to sleep in late. I was very routine with Joshua & Jeremiah's bedtimes and wake-up times during the week. On Saturdays, I was hoping they had a little internal clock that would tell them it was not time to wake up yet! But just like clockwork, my two little ones were up bright and early on a Saturday and Sunday morning ready for breakfast. Now that they are a bit older, they still wake up early, but they will not always wake me. There is hope for those single moms who still have little ones.

One of the areas I realized early on was that being single, and parenting can be extremely tiring – especially when you are the custodial parent. My days typically start no later than 5 a.m., and they do not end until after 9:00 p.m. Before I leave home in the morning, I usually prepare breakfast, lunches, do chores, and whatever else I can fit in. My mornings and afternoons are filled with commuting, and so there are two-hour blocks of time where I must remain alert for travel. The Uber app is an attractive choice each day, wishing I had someone to drive me to work!

Amid all we do as single moms, rest tends to get put on the backburner. On Monday, we think, "I'll get my rest on Saturday."

But there are five whole days to function before then. One year I decided to get me a second job around the holidays at a large retail store in the mall to make some extra money for gifts. I was doing my full day's work as a Manager. Then in the evenings, I transformed into a cashier scanning beautiful clothing and trying to explain to customers why a coupon was no longer valid (smile). Things were going well for the first 2 – 3 weeks, but around week four, my body was not too happy about all the new standing and walking I was doing. I drove home and called my son and father out to get me. I could no longer even walk by the time I got back.

The problem was not that I didn't have the stamina to do the extra job. This issue was I was not getting enough rest to balance all that I was doing. This condition is not an uncommon problem among women – and particularly single parents. I have watched my mom work as a nurse for long hours and sometimes more than one shift as I grew up to make ends meet. As the oldest child, I spent my afternoons taking care of my two little sisters. Some mornings I would have to comb their hair. My sisters still tell stories of how I wasn't the gentlest hair comber (yikes!). I combat that story with the fact that I was only 10-years-old and had no clue how to comb a 4-year-old's hair gently. I just wanted to help my mom as she continually found the strength to "make it happen" each day. And I've walked that same road, but the question is at what cost? Is it at the expense of high blood pressure, chronic fatigue, and diminishing mental health?

Come to me, all you who are weary and
burdened, and I will give you rest.
—Matthew 11:28

Rest is ceasing work or movement to refresh, relax, or recover strength. There is a keyword here – "recover." We wake up each day with an element of strength, but as the day progresses, strength begins to deplete. By the end of the day, we are not the same person we were in the morning. If you work overnight, then typically, your strength is depleted by mid-day the next day. If you are not able to have a real-time recovery, then you are not resting. Resting is not always sleeping. When I graduated recently, I brought myself a recliner as a graduation gift and put it in my room to become a part of my routine. I may not always lie in bed, but if I sit in my recliner and read, I am still resting in some form. Our bodies need the time and attention that the rest offers it.

Now, I will confess I am not an expert at rest. I have an issue at times with putting a whole lot on my plate and leaving little time to rest. As a single mom, I have become so used to "doing" all the time. Very rarely ever "being." If a Saturday is free, I will look for something to fill it in! Trampoline parks, arcades, and parks know me very well as I always seek to keep my children entertained. But each day I am learning to get better in this area. And realizing that my children need rest too – whether they believe it or not. Single parenting tends to leave you heavily focused on the present moment. Because you are the primary breadwinner, caregiver, and housekeeper – there is always a task that needs your attention. Yet, the reality is that if we do not rest, we will not have the stamina to remain diligent in the long term.

Now that my sons are in 6th and 7th grade, I have begun to think about being there for life events like high school graduations and, hopefully, weddings and grandchildren someday! The only way that I will be able to withstand the season is through resting now. It doesn't mean I can stop working and taking care of life. But what it does mean is making choices about what I say "YES" to in my life. Saying "YES" is not always an answer to a request from others on the outside. Many times, we say "YES" to ourselves. I have said "YES" to myself when I stayed up all night worrying about things that will not change with an ounce of worry. I've said "YES" to myself when I make entertainment promises to my children that they never even asked me for – only to try to make up for things that are not even missing. I have said "YES" to allow my past to overburden my thoughts rather than looking towards the future as I should have.

Saying "YES" to the areas of your life that you should not, can cause you to be in a place of drainage and little satisfaction. I have signed up for tasks that I thought would be so fulfilling, only to find that it wasn't all it was cracked up to be because I was over-extended. When you are over-extended, whether naturally or spiritually, it's hard to enjoy the moments, that's why depression is so powerful because it over-extends the emotion to a place where nothing else can seem to bring any joy. But when you learn to carry your designated process in that season, you will find much more fulfillment in what you were doing.

Ever since I was about sixteen years old, I have been active in ministry in various forms – singing, preaching, serving, and titles. I have traveled on singing tours to Switzerland, Belgium, and Germany. I've experienced the ability to be everywhere and go everywhere! You plan it, and I was there. But when I fell ill during pregnancy and became the mom of a preemie, my life changed dramatically. Many of the activities that I had in my life seemed to have faded away more quickly than I could say goodbye. As I look back now, I had to stop then so I could be where we are now. God knew that my journey would take me this way.

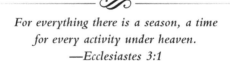

For everything there is a season, a time
for every activity under heaven.
—Ecclesiastes 3:1

For many years, I felt disqualified – like life had moved on without me. I looked around and saw so many progressing in careers, love, and ministry. But when I look at my two boys, I don't ask "why" anymore. I realize that they were my "why." I had to stop so I could take care of them, and indeed they are my greatest blessing. When I see my son Jeremiah playing basketball, that was diagnosed at birth to potentially not walk; it drowns away any question of why I had to say "No" to myself and "YES" to my journey. When I see Joshua towering over me at the height of 5'8" despite being a two-pound baby, it reiterates the "YES" to my journey. Your sacrifice will never go unnoticed. As I write these words, my tears fall. We must understand the importance of rest so that the weariness will not take over our lives and shadow the journey ahead.

Even if I were married tomorrow, the part of me that has been shaped as a single mom would never be removed. I'll always have this passion because I understand the journey. A ring does not change the 10+ years of single parenting. I am who I am because of this journey. This journey is my life. So, I admonish rest for all who I will encounter as I tell this story.

After I gave birth to my first son, I developed post-natal hypertension. My blood pressure remained elevated for many years despite various medications. The only time I saw my blood pressure controlled was during the pregnancy of my second son. After birth, hypertension returned and has followed me over the years, and there were seasons where I have been on large amounts of medication, and my blood pressure still would not come under control. The fact that I had hereditary indicators did not help. It was not until I started to evaluate my life that I could find the correct therapies and have even been taken off some medications. My prayer is that someday I will not need any medicines.

One standard indicator in my regimen was lack of rest. Because of a lack of rest, my body (and mind) did not have adequate time to digest the day. There is much that happens during sleep, and it is vital to our schedules! Sometimes single parents take on extra jobs, which can even further takeaway time to rest. The key is to do your best to create a time of rest. Not just for your physical body but your mind as well. Over the past few years, I have cut back on eating fast food to be healthy and to have extra money to treat myself to a massage periodically! Just laying there and being relaxed is so beneficial for the body. I do not necessarily fall asleep, but in that dark and quiet room, I find serenity as the tension in my body is removed through massage therapy.

Tension is another side effect of the lack of rest in our bodies and our homes. When you don't have rest, then you don't have patience.

Having two active boys has required patience beyond human capabilities at times! My oldest son Joshua has always struggled with sleep. He came home from the hospital on a sleep apnea monitor and has been on a Continuous Positive Airway Pressure (CPAP) machine since he was three years old. When he was smaller, he required being held every night and rocked to fall asleep. No matter what I was doing, I had to stop to rock Joshua. Gratefully, Jeremiah was a very easy-going baby and would settle for just watching me rock and coax Joshua to sleep each night. As Joshua grew older, bedtime became more of a competition, and he would act out tremendously at bedtime. Many evenings I did not know how I would make it thru! I wanted to sleep, and he didn't. By the time I would finally win the battle to get him to sleep, I was drained, guilty about getting upset, and exhausted from it all.

Then one night, I got this idea that if that calming music in a small room for a massage could bring me down off the high horses of anxiety I was on – maybe it would help Josh. I found a YouTube video with the sound of piano and rain on my phone and Iaid it next to him for the first time one night. I can still remember going into the room he shared with his brother and putting the phone down on the wooden tray table that held his CPAP machine. I said, "Josh, Mommy found you some music for bedtime, and let's listen." I remember pressing play that night and pressing play on that video for many, many more nights to come. That music signaled rest, and my phone was off-limits to me or the world from 8:00 p.m., so he could tune in and listen. This method is just one of the many tactics I had to find to create rest in my life and my children's lives. But all these years later, I can genuinely say I am getting better. Buying a recliner for myself was a sign of my understanding that it is important to "sit down somewhere."

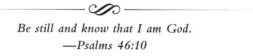

Be still and know that I am God.
—Psalms 46:10

Still in the noun form means deep silence and calm. When I hear "deep" silence, it makes me understand that being still does not mean being quiet. It means being quiet long enough to go beneath the surface. Along with rest, I put a heavy focus on my nutrition and was able to shed over 50 pounds over the last ten years and maintain weight loss. I've watched my level of sodium intake and ensure to get enough fruits and vegetables. One of the areas that I find a struggle at times is getting those nutritious meals on the table because of the hectic schedule of being the sole home leader. Sometimes after a long day, the drive-thru of a restaurant seems more feasible than making a meal. But I have consciously focused on reducing eat-out nights to at least 1-2 times a week. I have coined Friday nights as family nights, and we pick a restaurant to go out and have dinner. This mindset makes the eat out night distinct and meaningful. If possible, I try to turn off all electronics so we can pay attention to each other. It makes a world of difference! The better I eat, the better I feel, and ultimately the better I sleep, resulting in the ability to refresh overnight for the next day.

When I rest, I can find more than just my worries. I can see myself underneath all the hustle and bustle. It's not uncommon to lose yourself as you give your all to be a parent. It would be best if you had time to be aware, so that you can navigate the journey successfully. Rest allows you to refuel and recharge for days ahead of you for your life and the life of those who mean the most: your greatest blessings.

But those who trust in the Lord will find new strength.
They will soar high on wings like eagles. They will run
and not grow weary. They will walk and not faint.
—Isaiah 40:31

7

Corporate Ladder in One Hand – Baby in Other

We all do not get to climb the ladder holding each level with both hands. Some of us must climb with strength in one hand while using that same strength to keep something precious in the other.

I obtained my first real job at fifteen-years-old at the International House of Pancakes, or better known as IHOP. I lived in the Bronx and IHOP, was across a bridge into Westchester County. The significant part about this bridge was it had sides for pedestrian walking, so I was able to cross the bridge with the traffic zooming past me safely. As I looked back, I realized there were no real guardrails between me and the cars as they passed. The only guardrail was on the opposite side to prevent me from falling over as the bridge reached higher heights and then sloped down into the next town over. Due to my age, the only position I was able to get was a hostess role. I stood at the door, greeted people as they came and left, and led them to their seats to enjoy a meal. My primary focus was to make sure that they sat down with the essential ingredients to their meal – a utensil set and a menu. And let's not forget a smile. I worked at IHOP for over a year until my mom decided to relocate to New Jersey.

When I was sixteen years old, my single mother stepped out on faith and brought her first home in Somerset, New Jersey. It was in a beautiful suburban neighborhood. We had a huge living room with a fireplace and over five bedrooms. This move was a dream come true for my sisters as we finally had our rooms! My room was downstairs, and my mother had a beautiful master bedroom upstairs with a balcony and walk-in closet. I saw the pride on my mother's face as a single parent when she drove us there for the first time. Just two years ago, I was able to share the same moment as I drove my sons to our first real home that I could call my own.

My sisters had a connected room upstairs. It was a unique build because you had to walk through one room to get to the other. To top this all of we had an above ground pool in the back. This was indeed something out of a movie for us! My mother worked so hard, and she was finally seeing the fruit of all her labors. I was so excited about this new start in life. I remember my first day walking into Franklin High School in Somerset, New Jersey, as the new girl from the Bronx. I still had my New York girl flair and style from being there in the Bronx, and it showed. I had a stark New York accent that was hard to ignore. I missed my family in New York, but I loved my new life with my mom and sisters.

My mother decided to take us to a local church not too far from home. She has always been a strong woman of faith and always ensured to keep us grounded in the church. Our church home in the Bronx was too far to commute to every Sunday. The new church in our neighborhood had a vibrant youth service on Fridays and, I started to attend. One evening an older woman joined us and introduced herself as the Director of the Board of Social Services there in town. She shared with us that they host a summer camp each year and that if we wanted a job, she would have interviews on that upcoming Saturday morning. I was immediately drawn to this elegant woman. I saw such a beautiful soul and love for youth that it pulled me in right away.

That Saturday, my mother had to work at her hospital in New York. She was still commuting to the city. I told her about the interview, and she said she thought it was a good idea and that I should walk over there that morning. I looked in my closet and pulled out what I thought was my best outfit. Looking back now, I cringe at my clothing selection. During that time in the '90s, patent leather clothing was in style. I showed up that morning for my interview at the Board of Social Services in a shiny black patent leather skirt and jacket and topped it off with Black patent leather shoes! Oh, I am so glad, this amazing Angel I was going to meet was able to look past my outfit and see my potential.

Don't let anyone think less of you because you are young.
Be an example to all believers in what you say, in the
way you live, in your love, your faith, and your purity.
—1 Timothy 4:12

I believe that day marked the beginning of my corporate journey. I was the only one who showed up to be interviewed that morning. The Director decided that she would not wait until summer to hire me. She said she needed someone to come by afterschool to type her letters for people in the community. I would come after school and sit at the big monitor with a blue screen and type out letters as she dictated right there in her office. Sometimes she would write it out and leave it there for me. In the summer, I worked as a camp counselor watching over small children who came to the camp in the summer. We did not have a lot of physical space there at Social Services, but it was a popular place for all the children in the summer.

Our Director always made sure it was safe and that the children were fed well. One summer, I was able to assist with the hiring process for the summer workers! I got my first taste of interviewing during that job and even worked as the intake for adult welfare recipients as I got older. I am forever indebted to the opportunities I received at a young age. I remained working there until I was finished with high school and walked away with a new level of professionalism, passion for the community, and expertise in written communication.

After this, I worked for different corporations, some in retail, others corporate based. By the time I was twenty-three years old, I was entering the health insurance industry. When I started with my current organization, I was getting married and starting my career. I started at the front-line position processing claims. Within two years, I was elevated to a Senior Representative assisting other representatives as well as handling supervisory calls. Not long after that, I was in the role of Assistant Supervisor and then Team Leader. During my career, I went through the breakdown of my marriage and the daunting reality that my life was changing.

I remember my boss at the time being aware of how life was changing for me. During my meeting with her, she told me how much she respected me continuing to remain steady during a significant loss. I took time off when needed and remained focused on the day to day of my career. When my son was born prematurely, I was out of work for a designated time to be there for him. I'm so glad I was able to work for a company that understood the importance of Family Medical Leave and maternal care. I was able to sit at my son's incubator in the NICU without worry and concern that my job was on the line. My health insurance covered all expenses.

When I returned to work after Joshua was born, I once continued pursue my leadership career. Another role became open, and I interviewed for the position and continued my journey. By the time I was eight years into my career, I was divorced with two small children. I did not always have a lot because I was the sole breadwinner, but I still showed up for work – ready and willing to give my best. Because of my desire to keep pressing forward, I was able to help others in similar situations, stay focused, and push during their times of uncertainties.

My motto has always been that if you remain diligent and dependable for 98 percent of the time, that the small two percent of the time when you need to make sudden changes, will not seem as impactful. Now, as a leader, I still materialize this motto in my career life by scheduling as much as I can in advance. I make appointments for my children ahead of time and schedule my time off or early leave to accommodate this. I don't call out of work unexpectedly except in extreme family emergencies or unexpected illness. My goal is to minimize the unscheduled to allow room for the "life happens" moments.

In the same way, let your light shine before others, so that they may see your good works and give glory to your Father who is in heaven.
—Matthew 5:16

I had to tell the story of where I began in my career journey because it's important to look back and see what has shaped us into the individuals we are today. At this time, I have now gained over sixteen years of leadership experience in both corporate environments and ministerial roles. My journey has allowed me to experience passion in leadership, and in the work I do with healthcare. I understand that I work with and serve people that may have a real issue and needs practical solutions. I did not allow my single parenting to become a crutch; instead, it has been the fuel that keeps me going even when I feel weary.

As a single parent, I realized I can still pursue my career. In one of my previous books, I told the story of how I wore the same black pumps for an extended period because it was all I had. I always kept at least 1 – 2 suits for essential meetings and ensured to have business casual clothes for regular office days. I remember going out and buying myself a new outfit when I had interviews and having to bargain hunt on clearance racks. It was humbling, but I never gave up.

In the end, that humility helps me to see people for who they are as I lead. I realize they all have homes that they maintain. Some have children they must feed and put through college. And some have already lived this walk and look towards retirement. Servant leadership helps me not to miss the opportunities to show compassion to those around me. Now I am learning the art of leading other leaders, and it is rewarding. I have gained extensive knowledge in a long-standing industry and continue to pursue additional learning in the interim. I am climbing with one hand holding my babies. No matter what, I cannot leave them behind. They are the blessings to fuel me forward.

At one point, with two little ones in daycare, the cost of my childcare expense was $400 per week! I wondered if it made sense to work, putting out over 80 percent of income to my onsite work childcare. But the sacrifice was well worth it as I was able to see my children during their infant years and toddler years. It was a proud day when Joshua walked into his first day of free preschool. I had an 8 a.m. start time at work and started at 6 a.m. each morning to be ready for drop-off at two different childcare locations.

During their elementary years, I found a fun summer camp that was close to a train station. For many summers, I took the train to work and left my car close to camp to ease the mileage. The kids knew if they heard the train come in around 4:30 p.m., Mommy was most likely on that train. There was an ice cream truck that sat outside of the camp every day, which set me up to have to buy them an ice cream cone every day. Oh, how we love those ice cream trucks! But it was the least I could do after they waited patiently for me all day at camp.

I can't pretend that I did this flawlessly every day without complaint! I would not be telling the truth if I did not say it was rough – most of the time! I cried, kicked, and screamed more than I wanted to over these years of trying to balance home and work. One day I seemed to be at my peak of it all and breaking. I called my mom from the room of my apartment, and I was on my knees. I said, "Mom, I can't do it. I just can't do it. I can't raise these boys on my own." I was crying from a deep place within my soul. A place that only God can touch in those moments. I kept saying, "I can't do it; I can't do it." And my mom kindly said back to me, "You can, and you will do this, Nikki." Those few words of confidence and command at the same time was just what I needed.

I've had that moment and others throughout the years. It's been an extreme balancing act. Whether you are single or married, being a parent has a cost with no price tag. That is because, for all its costs, it is worth is priceless. I can't wait to get home to my sons every day. I can't wait to see them in the mornings when they wake up. My oldest son is taller than me now, and I sit and stare at him in awe. Over the years, when I felt like I was going to break, I would think about them and realize how much they depend on me. And that keeps me going. I've learned how to find some element of balance with my children and my career. There is no secret formula for this. You have or will find your formula. The key is to be intentional in looking for that formula, so the years do not pass by, and you have not been able to enjoy the moments. Next, we will talk about the extreme balancing act - finding "You" with all the balls in the air.

8

EBA – *Finding "You"* *with all the balls in the air*

Balance is about creating a synergy with hopes of
evening out the playing field of all things in progress.

You may be wondering what EBA stands for? It's a new term that I created to describe my life at times. EBA stands for Extreme Balancing Act. But what is balance? It is not uncommon to hear the word balance being spoken about. From home life to work life, a balance has been identified as this mysterious aspect that allows us to keep all the balls in the air. But what is balance? Is it a focused effort or something that I need to keep in mind as I go about my normal day-to-day life?

For the past two years, I have focused on multiple areas of life that I felt were God-inspired and vital to my life. On any given day, I worked 8-10 hours, came home to my two young children under thirteen, and then stayed up late at night and woke up early to finish graduate school homework with hopes of finishing. I realize that I have been "balancing" all of this for many years. I think the most extreme aspect of my balancing act was the day I became a single mom of a 5-month-old and 26 -month-old.

According to Merriam Webster, balance is "an even distribution of weight enabling someone or something to remain upright and steady" (m-w.com). Let's break down this definition:

Even: flat and smooth; equal in number amount of balance
Distribution: the action of sharing something out among a number of recipients
Of: expressing relationship between a part and a whole
Weight: the body's relative mass or the quantity of matter contained in it, giving rise to a downward force; the heaviness of a person or thing.
Enabling: giving (someone or something) the authority or means to do something.
Someone: a person
Something: a thing
To: expressing motion in the direction of (a particular location); approaching or reaching
Remain: continue to exist, especially after other similar or related people or things have ceased to exist.
Upright: sitting or standing with the back straight; strictly honorable or honest.
And: used to connect words of the same part of speech, clauses, or sentences, that are to be taken jointly.
Steady: firmly fixed, supported, or balanced; not shaking or moving.

This definition is loaded with meaning as you break it down. You may be able to relate to this desire to create balance in our lives in some shape or form daily. In looking back over my life, I realize I started my extreme balancing act early. I had homework, younger sisters, and a single mom who worked as a nurse. Thankfully, I still lived in the cocoon of our three-family brick home, where my grandmother lived on the top floor and served as a staple of support for all of us. At that time, I shared a small room with my two younger sisters, and I already had a desire to make some difference in my life – at the cost of my balance. It was possibly starting so early in the workforce that it shifted my maturity faster than it should have-one small check leading to the desire to have more, to create more, to live more.

It's no one's fault – not even mines. We live in a society where we are always juggling so much more than we really must, thereby losing some of the ability to perfect a few meaningful things. This topic of the extreme balancing act has been on my heart as my awareness heightened around this topic. It's not uncommon to have a conversation with one of my sisters and bounce from topic to topic. We talk about kids, our jobs, our mother, our fathers, our health, our brains, our emotions- the list can go on and on. This conversation is not necessarily loaded just because we are sisters. It is loaded because that is just how much we have going on at the same time.

Sometimes, it is at the expense of our health as we try to juggle. Exercise routines become New Year's resolution and soon fade out. New eating plans become overridden by the need to get something quick, fast, and in a hurry. We are tempted daily to keep all the balls up in the air – sometimes to appear to have it all together. Being a single mom and career woman, I was always conscious of the perception that some ball would fall simply because I did not have another person to catch them. I had the balls of before school and after school arrangements in the air. Also, weekend and extracurricular activities were in the middle. And let us not forget sleeping and eating. The balls are unending! After a while, I was more focused on perception than I was focused on reality. The reality was I was drowning with all the balls in the air.

Remember that balance is defined as an "even distribution." My first encounter with the concept of "even" had to be in grade school as I learned about numbers. Learning about even versus odd numbers is not possible until you have the basics of counting. My two-year-old niece has mastered the ability to count already, and some numbers may even be spoken in Spanish (or baby-talk!). However, if I ask her to tell me which number is even, she cannot do that. Her mind has not yet grasped the concept of the figures having the ability to have remainders. An even number means that it can be divided by two and have no remainder left over. I can recall as a young girl shouting out "2, 4, 6, 8, 10" and so on in class as we recited our even numbers. I always felt like odd numbers were harder to deal with in division. Why did that that one have to be leftover as I tried to divide seven by the number two? I hear you saying, "Nikki, this is not math class!" But for a moment, I wanted us to journey back into the original concept of even versus odd as we seek to balance our lives.

Even ground, even numbers, even hours bring about a sense of equality and smoothness to our lives. When our lives are off balance, there is usually this "leftover number" hanging out there that we need to capture to bring it back into balance. Imagine you approach a beautiful green pasture of grass – you are looking forward to spreading a blanket and enjoying a nice lunch in the sun. As you venture into the grass, you learn that the land is uneven. Some parts are high, and others are low. You attempt to layout your lunch, but your basket is lopsided. You cannot lie in the sun as you would expect to do because the uneven land proves to have your head extended back with your back off-line, and your legs cannot get comfortable. You decide to make the most of it simply because you are there. The imbalance does not cause you to pack your lunch up and look for another way. Instead, you find a way to find comfort in the imbalance.

Balances were used in biblical days to measure weights. It consisted of two pans attached to a balancing beam. The beam was suspended by a cord, ring, or hook in the center. Balances could also be held by hand. Balances were an essential part of economic life because money was weighted during this time in gold and silver. For every business transaction, money had to be weighed. This is a vast difference in how we present our money for payment today in dollar denominations we add together. The Bible even speaks regarding balances in Leviticus 19:36, stating, "Use honest scales and honest weights, an honest ephah and an honest hin. I am the Lord your God, who brought you out of Egypt (NIV)." One of the pitfalls of balances is they could be easily manipulated, so God warns against this by saying use "honest weights."

It is hard to imagine using a balance scale to purchase items at a store in our current life but, this is precisely what we do as we bring all our tasks, desires, and dreams into one place. We attempt to find even ground amid it all. So how can we "even" out our lives to achieve the much-desired balance? The answer is in the balance itself: We must assess the weight of what we carry to determine if we are out of balance.

Therefore, since we are surrounded by such a huge crowd of witnesses to the life of faith, let us strip off every weight that slows us down, especially the sin that so easily trips us up. And let us run with endurance the race God has set before us.
—Hebrews 12:1

If you are like me; you have may have tried a weight loss program at some point or another. I can recall trying the Weight Watchers Program about two years ago, which is a phenomenal program. I watched women be empowered to shed weight they have been carrying for years. I seemed to be following all the points systems, but when I stood on the scale, it showed no difference! After a few meetings, I decided to sit back and be aware of how I was handling the program.

Interestingly, after I stood on the scale, the disappointment of not losing weight did not motivate me. It resulted in me eating more! The stressor and emotion of missing the mark on the scale resulted in my subconsciously turning to my comfort foods (cakes, French fries, etc.). This stressor ultimately caused me to gain additional weight – the opposite of what the program intended for me. I had to learn how to balance out the fluctuations in my weight and still stay the course. Once I focused on it mentally, it made a big difference for my success in the program.

Unnecessary weight can cause things to fall out of balance. Diabetes and heart attacks have become commonplace in our world today. Some of us have dealt with this ourselves and have family members who have suffered from this or know firsthand what it is to have these conditions. The dominant force in our healthcare system currently is prevention. Almost any prevention program you encounter for these types of chronic conditions mentions weight loss as one of the starting points for prevention. Diabetes.org is a website dedicated to understanding the disease and indicates that weight loss of 10-15 pounds could make a difference for those affected. My goal is certainly not to drill you regarding losing weight physically. Instead, we need to be aware of the extra weight we carry mentally and emotionally, which prevents us from experiencing.

For many years, I really couldn't find "Me" amid all the balls in the air. There were times I added balls to boost my self-worth. It was as if I felt the more balls in the air – the more important it would make me. The more balls I had up in the air, the more stories I could share about my exhausting life as a topic of conversation. But all those balls only left me with extreme burnout with no real direction. I was busy but not moving forward. Where was my 5-10-year plan? I woke up one day asking who Nikki was and what her plan was. I was living, but it was just survival, not the abundant life God promised me. As I started to lay down the balls over the past few years, I've been able to get in touch with my inner spirit and soul. The soul is the seat of our emotions. It is where we feel and thrive. It's not enough to be busy with life but not tending to the soul. My balance was in the even distribution of the weight on my heart, mind, and body.

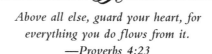

Above all else, guard your heart, for
everything you do flows from it.
—Proverbs 4:23

When I walked out of the hospital with my preemies, doctors, and nurses warned me that premature babies tended to be strong-willed because they start life-fighting to live. They don't know that we are all there praying for them. All they know is they want to keep breathing. They gave me a foretaste that the toddler years may show this and, yes, it did! At a certain age, I decided to take my oldest son to behavioral therapy. I needed strategies to curb some of his strong will or ways to cope with myself! I was feeling frustrated with parenting on most days. My character is to be more relaxed and laid back, so I was a "mom" figure. But trying to be a mom and dad at the same time – I struggled with switching roles for discipline.

As I grew in my process, I learned that I didn't have to switch roles. I just needed to focus on being me and laying down the rules and boundaries in our home and sticking to it! We had our first official meeting with the counselor, and I proceeded to tell her why I was there with Joshua in the room. She talked to Joshua at his level to understand what was going on and explained my concerns. We spent another session talking about strategies that we would set in place to help both of us. At this point, Joshua was about eight years old, so his ability to create full-fledged plans was not there yet. But something happened in the third session. I arrived as usual, but she had a chair for Joshua at the outside of the door and one chair for me inside. I can still see the moment she looked at me and said, "Now, let's talk about you."

For the next few weeks, we transitioned to focusing on the balls in the air concentrating on me and how I was doing. It had been a few years since I sat down with someone besides my family and trusted friends. When I was divorced initially, I met with a divorce counselor who helped me position what was happening in my life. I felt like this set-up was part two of looking in and embracing where I was at this point.

For once, I had to admit that I secretly wished for my white picket fence with a dog, children, and handsome, caring husband. We would have no bills and no worry in the world except to love each other. While some of this vision was possible, it's not the stark reality. I had to come to grips with my current state. I reached out for help to juggle the parenting ball, and in turn, I was given support to look within and find "me" in all the balls in the air. Those balls defined me, but as they fell, it was sad to see that none of "me" was in those balls. I have had many experiences like that over the years, in which God set up divine appointments that I did not ask for but was needed.

I am now over ten years into single parenthood and taking care of myself. My children are just five years from the first day of college, and I am preparing financially and emotionally. All these matters of the heart are like balls that create my balance or imbalanced act. I find that when I put each concern in its proper place, each task in its appropriate time, and my heart in its rightful place, that it all seems to balance out more than I thought. In all you do, there is still "YOU."

9

When the Money is Funny

Financial freedom is not all about having
more money. A part of financial freedom is
breaking away from habits and mindsets that are
counterproductive to the freedom we desire.

I'll never forget the day I moved into my first apartment as a single mom. Since I was married at an early age, I had never actually lived on my own. For the first year and a half after divorce, I lived in the Bronx with my mother and family to have a support system. But after long commute days from New York to New Jersey, I decided to launch out on faith and move back to New Jersey closer to work. When I told my mother I was leaving, she was so worried. "Nikki, what if you can't do it by yourself?" was the question she kept asking me. I reassured my mother that I could make it out there on my own, packed up the little I had, and moved to New Jersey.

When I moved into my apartment, I only had five possessions: air mattress, toddler bed, a green 1-seater couch, TV stand, and a used TV from a used furniture warehouse. I went to work each day and came home to turn on our little TV for my boys while I cooked us a meal. Then at night, I put my younger son in his red spiderman toddler bed, putting the older boy in the air mattress bed. It took a few weeks, but soon, our place started looking like a home. The first beds came as a gift from my mother for my boys. They were so excited. I can still see the blue sheet sets I brought for them to match in their room. I stayed on my air mattress until I was able to get ahead.

Don't worry about anything; instead, pray about everything. Tell God what you need and thank him for all he has done. Then you will experience God's peace, which exceeds anything we can understand. His peace will guard your hearts and minds as you live in Christ Jesus.
—*Philippians 4:6-7*

Someone I knew called and told me they were selling their home and had a living room set available if needed. I got a truck and called a friend to go with me. My friend was such a blessing to me that day. I came home with a living room set (which I kept for over five years) and plates and items for the kitchen. I felt so blessed and unashamed. At the time, I could not afford for pride to stand in the way of what I needed, which was a fresh start. The beginning of my years was made up of used items from various places. But the beauty is that it all came to create a space for me in my own home. When I came home each day, it was ours, and that is what mattered. I didn't have much money left over after child support and all living expenses, but I always made it my business to pay my bills on time. I knew that I had to remain credible because I was the primary source of my home.

Those years grew me up. I had to learn to make up the difference wherever I could. I had this habit of saving my loose change each day, and I cannot pretend like that change did not pay a bill sometimes! A whole lot of coins can pay a light bill! I had gotten used to having a husband to make those problematic creditor calls or negotiate. But I had to learn how to make those calls on my own and stand up for myself. Each time I was able to make some stride in my life, I would get a new place. Our life improved little by little, year by year. It took small calculated steps. My boys would say, "Mommy, can you buy us a house and give us our rooms?" I would look through the rearview mirror at their little faces in the back, and I would say, "Yes, Mommy is going to get you a house one day. I promise." It was like a rehearsed scene that happened at least once a week – and even more, as they got older.

I confess I did not always make the right and best decisions! Some financial decisions seemed smart at the moment but did not have a long-term benefit. For example, I went and brought a new car (with a lousy interest rate) and traded in my SUV truck instead of keeping it as a back-up. Yet, God never allowed me to run dry. There was paycheck to paycheck days that seemed close. But that money would always come as soon as the negative was going to hit. I spent nights laying over my bills and trying to get out of the red. Sometimes in tears. But I know that God was working on my character in those midnight hours so that one day, I would be able to tell this story. Not because I perfected it – but because I survived.

Recently I relocated to North Carolina and was able to fulfill that promise to my sons of buying them a home. We broke ground on our new home in the early spring. Not only was I able to buy them a new home, but it was really going to be "new." It would be a home that we would watch be built from the ground up. The day we went to look at the house and pick out a lot, my son put a part of his toy into the ground. It was as if he was claiming that space and land for us. He said, "Mommy, if I put this here, does that mean they will build the house on top of it?" I assured him there was a high possibility. I was still holding on to the faith that I would be able to bring this pass with God's help.

On a warm summer day months later, I closed on my new home! I looked down at the deed paperwork, and something it said repeatedly stood out to me. After every description of my name, it listed me as "A single woman." It was a declaration of the fact that I was doing this on my own. My father sat there with me at the table to witness the day of me doing something historical for our family. Immediately upon closing, I ran to pick up my boys and brought them to the site where we had been visiting for months as the home was built. Josh still talks about the fact that he knows that his toy is underneath our house forever. They ran into the empty house and rolled all over the living room. The joy on their faces was beyond measure. I took them to their designated rooms and gave them a tour. They tell me all the time they love it here.

I didn't buy the most extravagant house I could find because I always keep the mindset that I need to somehow live below my means. This mindset has been ingrained in me since I have learned what it is like for the "money to get funny." I have seen tremendous blessing in my career, and it has afforded me the ability to do things for my sons that I always wanted to do. They are my blessings. I live by the notion that God will continue to provide for me because I need to provide for them. My children understood what it meant for me to tell them no at times when I did not have it. They have watched me struggle, and do not have a problem if I bring home a pair of pants that are not a specific name brand. They learned how to have one pair of school shoes at an early age until I could buy the next pair. I bargain hunted and saved up for things.

As God allows "more" to enter my life, I can do "more" for them without creating the notion that it is a constant supply. I can see their gratitude peek through their childish desires. My son Joshua will go in his wallet and give me his allowance at times and say, "Mommy, you have it." I kindly give it back to him, reassuring him that I don't need it. It reminds me of the fact that they have journeyed with me. My prayer and hope are that their journey with me will cause them to be compassionate men who will give and love.

During the periods of stretching financially as a single mom, I found that there has been a tremendous benefit to be a giver. Giving does not always take the form of money. Giving can be in the shape of time, energy, prayers, and love. However, I have seen the fruit of the biblical concept of "Give and You Will Receive." Repeatedly, there have been times when I gave to others even when I was in need. I found ways to give and be apart of my local church and charitable organizations. I looked to provide service in some way through volunteering. There is a deep fulfillment of giving – even when the money is funny. I can provide an account of many times that I stepped out on faith and gave to someone else and then received that and beyond miraculously through unexpected blessings such as checks in the mail! They were surprising to me, but God had them already in progress. I just had to have enough faith to believe. Over the years, I learned that closing my hand was not the way to achieve more. Of course, in all things, I had to use wisdom as I navigated to ensure that I could maintain a roof over me and my children's head.

Give and you will receive. Your gift will return to you in full – pressed down, shaken together to make room for more, running over, and poured into your lap. The amount you give will determine the amount you get back.
—Luke 6:38

Another area that becomes important to navigate is debt as a single parent. I have learned that lesson more than once regarding the entrapment of falling deep into credit card debt and other areas. I also learned that it was good to have those lines of credit available only for emergencies. Seasonal emergencies like Christmas were not supposed to be the target for those plastic friends. But I can't say that I wasn't guilty of using credit to make Christmas happen. The key I have found is to look for those cyclical issues that would cause me to need to do that. Asking myself questions such as "How do you start to prepare in October?" and "What happens in November to change the course?" have been vital. Now, as my children are getting older, it is hard to go into the dollar store and get a bunch of little toys and wrap them. Now they want full-fledged trips to the mall as Christmas gifts!! Times have changed.

Another area I had to learn financially was to stop trying to over-compensate for being a single parent! There are times that I have made too many promises to my children that were not even necessary. I've always wanted them to feel like they weren't left out of life due to my pull to be mom, breadwinner, and everything else.

Weekends were filled with endless activities to different play places and playdates. Thankfully, the boys were close in age, so they have always had somewhat of the same interests in the same periods with just a little lag. When Joshua was getting into liking action figure toys, Jeremiah was slowly right behind him creeping to look at those cool action figure toys as well. So even when we didn't have a whole lot of family and friends around, I could take them out to the park to have fun with just the two of them.

One year for Jeremiah's sixth birthday, I came up with the grandest scheme ever. I was going to take them to Disney World for the first time as a surprise! I looked around for great deals on flight and hotel. We went to Georgia first so the destination would be closer and spent a few days there visiting with my mom at her vacation home. On the morning of his birthday, I raised them out of bed early and put them in the car with our bags. My mom got up as well to drive us to the airport in Atlanta, GA. Joshua and Jeremiah were sleepy and cranky (as a child would be at that time of the morning). On the way to the airport, I decided I would do the big reveal about where we were going. I said (in my happiest 6 a.m. voice), "Guess what boys?" I looked through the rearview mirror at their little eyes looking at me in the dark car. And just like on TV, I screamed out, "We are Going to Disney World!"

I waited for a second and realized I was the only one screaming. Joshua, who was eight years old at the time, and was always happy to be going somewhere, started squirming in his seat, and showed some excitement. But Jeremiah, the birthday boy, had this blank stare on his face. I said, "Jerry (his nickname), we are going to Disney World!" desperately trying again to stir up the television moment that I had imagined. In all his six-year-old innocence, he said, "Mommy, I didn't ask you to go to Disney World. I just wanted to go to Chuck E Cheese." Ok now, you can only imagine my heart dropped instantly. Just like yours probably did! He even cried because we were not going to Chuck E Cheese! At that moment, Jeremiah taught me a valuable lesson. See, he could barely understand what it meant to go to Disney World at that point. But my desire to rush the moment was more significant than my awareness of the Chuck E Cheese season we were in. I put myself into all that financial commitment when a $30 trip to Chuck E Cheese with a pizza and cake would have sufficed.

We went to Disney World that year because it was already scheduled, and I was not losing one dime. Their dad arranged to meet us there, and for a few days, we had a small family trip with them. It worked out perfectly because it turns out neither Jeremiah nor I do not like roller coasters! So, we sat outside of all the rides while Joshua and his dad screamed in the air on roller coasters. At some point, I ended up pushing Jeremiah in a stroller through Disney World that year. He was exhausted. Last year, five years later, I took them back to Florida, which was a different experience because it was the right timing.

This lesson and many other lessons taught me to be aware of my financial seasons and operate accordingly. I try to remain conscious that I am not pressing my desires on them. At times there were voids in my life, and because they were closest to me, I tended to include them in everything. They started going out to eat at restaurants at a young age because I had a desire to go out. I think it was just a date that I needed at the time, but I took my boys instead! And now, they are career restaurant eaters, often placing their orders before I can even look at the menu.

The money has gotten funny more often than I would want to count, but I have to say with my whole heart that God has never let me down. God keeps on providing and making way for my two boys and me in ways that I cannot even describe on these pages. From the day they arrived until now, I have never been forsaken. There were seasons where God would lay it on someone's heart to give to me, not knowing how much I needed it. I will never forget going to the store with $10 − $20 in my pocket and making it stretch. Child support was consumed by childcare bills and all the other things that came along with living day-to-day. Now I look for ways to be a blessing to others, and I will never forget each moment that I have walked. The funny money seasons made me better. The funny money seasons reminded me of how blessed I was – with or without. It allowed me to look at the blessings around me that had no price tag – my sons. They were more valuable than money could ever provide. That is my greatest blessing every day.

I want to encourage everyone who reads this book and experiences seasons of lack in their life. Scarcity does not always come in the form of money. Sometimes we lack emotional support. Sometimes we even lack love. But I admonish you - Don't give up. Speak to your situation. Don't hold your head down and drown in anxiety and worry.

The other day, I was taking a morning walk, and there was a bird in a tree. I couldn't help but to stop and look up because he was chirping so loudly. It's as if he was waiting right there for me. I took my phone out to capture his picture, but I turned on the video because I didn't want to walk away with just an image. I tried to walk away with his sound. His sound was what he had to share with the other birds and the world around him. I do not know what he was saying or if it had meaning. But I know that for me that morning it drove my heart to scripture that screamed aloud in my soul's crevices.

Therefore, I tell you, do not worry about your life,
what you will eat or drink; or about your body,
what you will wear. Is not life more than food, and
the body more than clothes? Look at the birds of the
air; they do not sow or reap or store away in barns,
and yet your heavenly Father feeds them. Are you
not much more valuable than they? Can any one of
you by worrying add a single hour to your life?
—Matthew 6:25-27

Worry has not been a stranger to me, and it is a battle that I have fought over the years and continue to fight. My journey with my boys started with trauma as they fought for their lives. I continued to operate in a flight or fight mode for many years as I went along my journey. My soul was extended to limits I cannot measure from dissolving a marriage and doctor's visits. My son said to me one day while we were sitting in the library, "Mommy, I worry sometimes, and I think I inherited that from you." I laughed because it was so unexpected, but my heart sank when he said it. That meant that he was able to detect my worry.

Worry is defined as giving way to anxiety or unease; allowing one's mind to dwell on difficulty or troubles. As you can see, I often refer to the definition of words because it brings so much revelation and understanding. Because of our human capabilities – difficulty or troubles will come to mind. But worry occurs when we dwell on pain or problems. It is when we "give way" to anxiety – meaning we let stress be in control. We can counteract our thoughts with positivity when worry settles in. When my son said that to me, it was a wake-up call that I needed to do a better job of how much I was letting worry take the wheel in my life and emotions. Now I use my commute time to work through my thoughts and concerns, so when I get home, I have processed some of those feelings and emotions and can have the emotional capacity for my children. If I must talk out loud in my car to process my thoughts – then I do that! The moral of the story is to do what you need to find some level of peace in your life – even when the money gets funny.

Not that I was ever in need, for I have learned how to be content with whatever I have. I know how to live on almost nothing or with everything. I have learned the secret of living in every situation, whether it is with a full stomach or empty, with plenty or little. For I can do all things through Christ, who gives me strength.
—Philippians 4:11-13

I've read this scripture many times over the years as a reminder that one of the greatest gifts I could have is contentment. I've had to digest it more than once because contentment is not always automatic. What is contentment? It is an inward state of satisfaction with what you have. It is not based on an outward expression but must be something that one embraces mentally to experience it. Contentment does not mean that I no longer pursue, instead, it indicates that I can enjoy where I am on the way to where I am going.

In this scripture, Paul shares that he knows how to live on almost nothing or with everything. He has experienced a full stomach as well as an empty stomach. Paul learned how to adjust based on his circumstances. As a single parent, there have been many adjustments based on my circumstances at the time. There were times where I had to decide to pay a bill or buy groceries. There were seasons with surplus where I may have been able to do something extra for myself, my sons, or someone else. In my earlier days, I remember being driven by material things: beautiful clothes, fancy pocketbooks, or even a nice car. But during my journey as a single mom, I learned what it meant to buy a purse that didn't have a name on it anyone would recognize. Instead, I looked for one with the right number of pockets so I could store things to help me organize. I tested the straps to see if it would not cause my shoulders any additional pain. As my seasons changed, my priorities changed. And re-prioritizing taught me how to be flexible with myself and my children. There were seasons where my sons wanted me to buy them something everywhere we went. Joshua and Jeremiah could find something they like even at the most desolate gas station! Whether it was a toy or a snack, they were never afraid to ask me for things. I always remained honest with them, and when it was not the right timing, I would say, "When Mommy gets paid, she is going to come back and get it for you." I would have to be specific on the exact day so they wouldn't ask me every day for a week! As promised, I would set aside funds and go back to get the item. I was teaching them that they cannot have all they want at the exact moment – some things they would have to save for and come back to get it.

Contentment does not indicate a poverty mindset. I propose it is the exact opposite. The poverty mindset will drive you to deplete all you have continually to feel satisfied. In contrast, contentment breeds the patience you need to wait for the right season. There is no one that you need to "keep up" with. For many years, I heard the term "Keeping up with the Jones's," indicating the mindset of trying to portray the image of others in your life. About halfway into single parenthood, I realized that I never met the Jones's and that I better try to keep up with myself!" You can be your own worst enemy if you are not willing to walk carefully through seasons. When great things happen in our lives, it can appear to happen suddenly to those on the outside looking in. For example, when this book is published, it will suddenly appear in the market for others to purchase and read. However, for every "suddenly" moment in your life, there are small calculated steps to get you there. Whether you realize those steps are happening or not.

The Lord directs the steps of the godly. He delights in every detail of their lives. Though they stumble, they will never fall, for the Lord holds them by the hand.
—Psalms 37:23-24

This journey has not been about having it all together for the world to see. I encountered a great woman of wisdom many years ago, and I asked her what kept her throughout all these years. She looked at me and said, "Character – its' who you are when nobody is looking." Those few profound words have stuck with me for over fifteen years. Walking through seasons of need is not about who is looking in at you; it's about your perception and ability to allow God to hold you by the hand. God is intrinsically concerned about every single detail of our lives. God is not just concerned about my heart, but I learned that God is also concerned about my finances.

Some of us have seen nothing but lack in our lives and learned at an early age that money was something that comes and goes. We may not have learned how to save and plan effectively. But what

I love about life is that if there is breath – there is hope. And it is never too late for you to grab hold of new ways of living and doing in your life. Psalms 37:24 acknowledges that we may stumble, but that the Lord will still hold us up by the hand. In the season when the money was funny, I learned to stop blaming it on the fact that I was a single parent. Instead, I decided to look in on the patterns in my life and learn to make the best of whatever I had – full or empty.

The gas tank has been low in my car, and the indicator said it was empty – but I never got stranded. I learned that there was always a little reserve there, even when it said it was empty. And so it is with our lives. When it feels like we are just about on empty, there is more there on reserve to push us through to our destination. And when the tank is full, there is satisfaction knowing we can go even further. In the "money is funny" seasons, humility comes to light, and your character is stripped and rebuilt. You see the world around you, realizing that it is only God's grace, which allows us to do all we can do. Those seasons made me a better worker as I realized that I couldn't take my employment for granted – that it was God's blessing to my sons and me. Those seasons made me learn how to share when I ate less so my boys could eat first and be filled. Those seasons brought me closer to God when I learned to get on my knees and pray to ask God for provision. I personally came to know the Lord as Jehovah Jireh – God who provides. I learned how to be content in whatever state I was in.

10

Faith — Not Fiction

When faith and hope intersect, it
creates the road to destiny.

Since I was a young girl, the concept of faith has been ingrained in the fabric of my being. I started out going to church early in life. My parents were divorced early on in my life, and I spent the summers down south in Tuskegee, Alabama, and winters up north in Bronx, New York. In the summers, when I went to visit my grandmother, I went to church at least 2 -3 times a week. My grandmother was a strong woman of faith, and I watched her remain faithful to God until her last days. She would put me in dresses and comb my hair, and we would sit on the porch waiting for the church van to arrive. It was the highlight of my day to jump on that van in the summer. I always made my way to the back to join the other kids. Thankfully, the church was a little way out of the main town, so it gave us some time to talk and joke. On the way back, we all fell asleep after our two-hour services.

During the winter, I would go to church with my mother, who is also a strong woman of faith. I was blessed to have my maternal grandmother in the home with us, so we all went to church together — grandma, mom, me, and my two little sisters. Sometimes we would convince my cousins to come along with us, and we looked like a small tribe walking in. We always dressed up on Sundays, and we looked forward to the good Sunday dinner when we got home from church. Grandma would start the meal early so that we would leave smelling the West Indian dishes from her native Jamaica brewing on the stove. I love the power of memory, which allows me to journey back to her kitchen in my mind 30 years later.

I watched my mother come through a difficult season of her life and give her life over to God. We read our Bibles daily, and I saw her transform right before my eyes. I still remember the day she went up to give her life to Jesus Christ wholeheartedly. She had been in the church all her life but had taken paths in other religions and world elements. As my mother's faith grew, my faith grew as a young woman. I felt a calling on my life at a young age but could not describe it. My mother saw this and continued to encourage me to stay the course. Being a young girl growing up in the Bronx was a challenge back then and still is now. By the time I was 14 years old, I was already beginning my journey of being caught into the street life. I started hanging with friends who were into drinking and smoking. Not before long, I was doing some of the very same things.

By sixteen years old, the hormones were developed and raging, and my friends and I spent nights down in Harlem at the hang-out areas like 125th street. I could write a whole other book about that season of my life! We took enormous amounts of risk going out on dates with strangers and riding trains late at night. During the '90s, drug trafficking was an epidemic in our neighborhoods, and it wasn't uncommon to be with someone who was a dealer. Tons of young men stood on corners and were captivated by the desire to have money and cars. Young girls were captive by the sight of young men in flashy cars symbolizing wealth. There was no real thought about saving for homes and obtaining education and assets. We were living in the moment!

Then one morning, my mother broke the news to me that we were going to New Jersey. I cried, but my soul rejoiced because this change was just what I needed to get me back on track. I would say from the time I was sixteen years old; I activated my faith in God and have been on this journey over twenty-five years later. Someone may ask, "If you had so much faith, why did you have to go through this journey you are on now?" My answer would be "Faith-not fiction." What is faith? Faith is the complete trust or confidence in someone or something. It is also defined as a system of religious belief.

Faith shows the reality of what we hope for; it is the evidence of things we cannot see. Through their faith, the people in days of old earned a good reputation.
—Hebrews 11:1

Faith is the element that allows me to trust and have confidence in God, who I cannot see. Faith pushes me to continue to keep growing and teaching me with hopes of drawing closer. Faith keeps me in a place of belief in healing when the doctor's report may say something different. Faith allows me to write these pages, never knowing who will read them, but trusting that the message is needed. My walk as a single mother has been driven by faith, even when I did not realize it. Over the years, I have had to remain steadfast. It does not mean that it has been a comfortable journey.

It would be fiction if I told you that I had this all figured out. It would be fiction if I wrote these pages, never confessing that my heart was broken more times than I could imagine. There have been unrealized hopes and dreams amid all the other great things that have happened. There have been lonely days and nights, even when there was a room full of people. There is a void that is created upon divorce, that then must be filled. But the stark reality is that life circumstances have warped some of your ability to trust and love again.

This journey has been a faith walk – with very little fiction. Years ago, my youngest son woke up one morning, screaming when he was two years old. I couldn't understand why he was so upset. I went to change his diaper, thinking maybe that was the issue. When I changed his diaper, there was a large bulging area in his groin, and when I touched it, he went into convulsions of pain. I rushed him to the emergency room, and within an hour, he was in emergency surgery for a hernia repair. Of course, I was an absolute mess as I always was when my children had to endure pain. I felt so bad for little Jeremiah. The doctor said they would observe him, and then we would be able to go home in a day or so. Well, that is not exactly how it turned out! Jeremiah started to run fevers for seven days straight. We could not leave the hospital until he was fever-free. This all happened within the same days as the courts finalized my divorce. It was pain on top of grief. It was faith, not fiction, that allowed me to believe that all of this would get better.

Over the years, I have been afforded the humbling opportunity to speak at church services, conferences, and, most of all, smaller servitude settings. I have learned that the non-fiction moments of my life are the driver for me being able to feel the hearts of others and share encouragement. I know what it is to be broken. I know what it is to miss the mark repeatedly. I understand looking into the mirror and only seeing mistakes instead of accomplishments. I know the struggle of trying to see yourself as beautiful and worthy of much more than you have been offered.

In my previous book, *Storm Clouds are Passing*; I make this statement in Chapter 5 of the book, which says, "Your reaction while the storm clouds are passing, will determine your condition when the sun shines again." How we handle the tough moments in life will make a difference in what we look like when it's all said and done. When I look at my two blessings, I see them flourishing and becoming awesome young men. I have not gotten it quite right in all my parenting, but I have always made a point to display faith when I could.

Faith is even more valuable when parenting through a crisis in your personal life or even in the world. A few years back, I was living in New Jersey during one of the worst hurricanes the state had ever seen. There was a tremendous amount of loss – life and property. The world seemed to stop, and suddenly, there was a shortage of food and gas as well as long lines to get to a bank teller machine for cash. We lost power for over a week. We used the light during the day and candles to get through the night. I was alone, but I had to rest in my faith that God was protecting us.

As I write this book, our nation is facing the COVID-19 pandemic, which has rocked the world's foundation. As I write this chapter, I just stood in a line at the local Walmart at 6 a.m. this morning hoping to get in and obtain food for my family as we quarantine on stay-at-home orders. The sight of empty shelves over the past few weeks has been mind-blowing. But even more than that, the sickness and death that has gripped the nation has been heartbreaking. My children are older now, and so they are very aware of what is happening. This moment is not fiction. It has become a faith walk.

My sons are subconsciously feeding on how I handle this time, both emotionally and spiritually. I have taught them the value of the time it takes and the risk I take in going out to get something as simple as food from the store, which was such a norm before now. But I've also allowed them to see me continue to pray and remain optimistic. I have openly turned down my plate in prayer and fasting on some days, so they understand that I am seeking God more than the comfort of my regular food. On Sundays, we sit in our living room and tune into our local church via YouTube so we can hear an encouraging message from our Pastor.

I had the humbling honor of my mother writing the foreword for this book. She is an amazingly strong woman of faith. It exudes from her whether you are with her in-person or by way of writing or telephone. She taught me how to get on my knees when times were rough, and my faith was weak. She always led by example. I love to read fiction and even enjoy writing fiction. But one concept about a novel is that although the characters may be fictional, the experiences within the book are usually ones that could occur in real life. You will have experiences, but the key is how you will respond and react to those experiences. For me, faith has been the key.

Truly I tell you, if you have faith as small as
a mustard seed, you can say to this mountain,
"Move from here to there", and it will move.
Nothing will be impossible for you.
—Matthew 17:20

The mustard seed is a tiny seed of various types of mustard plants. Mustard seeds are known to be small but can grow quickly in the right conditions. Mustard seeds can also produce plants that are large as well. Faith may not always start robust and large, but as it is planted in the right heart conditions – it continues to grow and flourish. Faith has been cultivated in my life is through prayer. Over the years, prayer transformed in my life from being something I did in a specific space and time. Yet, prayer became a constant in my thoughts throughout the day. Prayer is directly talking to God, so there is no limit to when and how I can do that. It's not always an outward appearance, but it may be a quieting within my soul.

During a difficult period of parenting, I would find myself bound by anxiety by even the slightest things my children did. I was already stressed out with all I had on my plate, and so it was not hard to tip me over the edge. One day I decided to bring prayer front and center to help me with coping. Every time my sons did something that would typically send me off the deep end – I would drop to my knees right in that exact moment and start to ask God to help me to remain patient and calm. As I dropped to my knees, each moment would diffuse the situation in my mind, and it would seem like less of an issue as the moments wore on. Then it had this amazing effect on my children as well!

The first time I dropped to my knees, they stopped right in their tracks to look at me on my knees. They were unsure about why I was stopping to pray at that moment. Over the next few times, they started to stop and kneel with me as well and took the opportunity to climb on my back too! The moral of the story is that I decided to replace the moments of frustration with moments of prayer instead. While they are older now, I still must pull that tactic out sometimes to get their attention.

We will use these stones to build a memorial. In the future your children will ask you, "What do these stones mean?" Then you can tell them, "They remind us that the Jordan River stopped flowing when the Ark of the Lord's Covenant went across." These stones will stand as a memorial among the people of Israel forever.
—Joshua 4: 6-7

Instilling faith in my children has been an important task as well. I realize that I first lead by example. I desire that they also will grasp their levels of faith in their lives. Joshua 4:6 -7 was an integral moment in the lives of the Israelites. God had miraculously allowed them to cross the Jordan River as a people. This was a major miracle! At that moment, God instructed Joshua to have twelve men go into the middle of the Jordan and gather one stone and carry it on their shoulders. These stones were to serve as a memorial for all that God had done in their lives. It was not meant for them to walk away from that moment in time without having some evidence of what happened in their lives. It was vital to show their children in the years to come as a sign of what God brought them through.

I don't have natural stones from all the years I have depended on God to carry me through – but the evidence I can display and instill is faith. It is not uncommon for Joshua and Jeremiah to talk to me about their faith. I have told them their story of their birth and all they have walked through to be able to recall God's faithfulness. We must continue to erect the memorials of faith in our lives so they can stand as beacons of remembrance that we made it through!

11

To Date or Not to Date…
That is the Question

*Dating with children is delicate and requires
thoughtfulness and patience. The key is following the
road signs along the way to get to the right destination.*

"Mommy, I want you to be married one day too." These few small words came from my oldest son a few years back while riding in the car. At this time, I was seven years divorced. I looked back at him through the rearview as I often did since they did not start riding in the front seat until recently (Josh still rides the back). I replied, "Thank you, baby, Mommy will be married one day too." I never quite knew why Josh said that on that night. We weren't on a conversation topic that would have sparked that conversation. We were coming from the YMCA, where I took them faithfully almost every evening to play while I exercised.

Possibly he looked at me driving home in our car that night and noticed the empty front seat. Maybe there was a tinge of loneliness on my face that evening that he could interpret in his young mind. But whatever it was – I remember the words being very comforting that evening. It was as if he was saying, "I want you to have someone mommy." Now, in reality, Josh usually wants the oxygen that I am breathing! He is my child that loves attention. If we are out at the pool, Josh is often the only one screaming across the pool, "Look Mommy!" as he jumps in and makes a splash with his thirteen-year-old body! Josh doesn't like to be alone much and has already stated that he is not going anywhere without his brother. I already sit and spend time wondering how I will ship Josh off to college in just five years.

So, when Josh spoke those words years ago, it was significant because it meant there was an opening on its' way in my life. When I became a single mom, my sons were still young. I had spent ten years in a marriage that was not going well for half of the marriage. We made a mutual decision to end the marriage with me doing all the paperwork to save money. I immediately jumped into creating a life for me, and my boys and dating seemed difficult. Thankfully, I lived with my mother for a bit, which afforded me some rare opportunities to catch a movie while the kids took an evening nap. My mother worked as a nurse at two hospitals, so her time and sleep were limited. Yet she always found a way to help me out with some free time when she could.

This chapter was probably the hardest to write. Not long after the divorce, my counselor, who I connected with for that season, asked me a straightforward (and loaded) question. We were wrapping up towards our last session, and she asked me, "Nicole, where do you see yourself in the next five years?" I recall it was an early summer evening because the office was still lit by sunlight even though it was late in the evening. I asked my sitter to keep the children a little later, so I could meet with my counselor every two weeks. This was an excellent move and helped me process all the changes happening in my life.

I proceeded to answer her question and started first with the ages of my children. I can't recall it exactly, but I'm sure it went something like this – "So in five years, Joshua will be seven, and Jeremiah will be five. I look forward to them being out of preschool. I don't anticipate having much more freedom, but I'm sure things will be a little easier. Oh, and I hope to have finished school and moved up in my company by then. I also hope to be back on track doing things in ministry again, where my passion lies. The boys will be a little more manageable by then."

She stared at me with this blank look. I was only telling her all the things we discussed prior. She wanted me to come from a deeper place. She wanted me to dig deeper into Nikki's soul and decide what it will look like in five years. So, she popped the follow-up question on me, "And what about love?" My heart started racing, and it was my turn to give her a blank stare. Oh no lady, please don't bring up the L word. I mean, I like the "L" word, and I live it all the time, but do not ask me about the romantic side of this word. My life is dedicated to my boys, I cannot see past where I am!

I did not dare to say all that (smile), so I decided to come up with something that I thought might get the conversation all wrapped up. I replied, "Mmmm in five years? I hope to have met someone nice by then, and even it would be nice to be married again." She took that answer and chewed on it. I think she decided to have mercy on me since it was our last session. She said, "Nicole, just be open to love in whatever form it shows up." I nodded my head in acceptance of that feedback and thanked her for all her help over the past few weeks as I processed my new beginning. I walked out of her office that day, never to return. But as I made it to my car, I had one observation – My reply did not mention the "L" word at all.

Love is patient and kind. Love is not jealous or boastful or proud or rude. It does not demand its own way. It is not irritable, and it keeps no record of being wronged. It does not rejoice about injustice but rejoices whenever the truth wins out. Love never gives up, never loses faith, is always hopeful, and endures through every circumstance.
—1 Corinthians 13: 4 - 7

Love has many definitions and comes in my shapes and forms in our lives. We love our children, we love our parents, and we love our families. We grow to love those we encounter, and they become extended family. Love is an intense feeling of deep affection. But it's not always just a feeling – it can also be a decision. I do not always feel like being a mom when I wake up each morning, but my decision to be there, coupled with my love for my children, keeps me going. Similarly, even when you are in a relationship, you do not always "feel" love, but your decision overrides the feeling and helps you continue the journey.

My mother and father divorced when I was a young girl, so I do not have a recollection of them being together in the same home. I only remember the effects of co-parenting, which afforded me the ability to have two homes. Since my father lived far away, I spent a lot of time with him on the phone each week. My mother had two additional children six and eight years after me, so I grew up with my little sisters. Since I was older, I learned to be responsible early on as my mother finished nursing school after returning home from the military. My mother worked long hours and went to school as well. But she always came home and made a meal for us. I watched her raise us on her own and struggle with love.

In the summers, I went to visit my family in the south and spent a lot of time with my grandmother, who was a widow. My grandfather passed when my father was a young boy, so I never got to know him. My grandmother was very resourceful. She worked at a restaurant as a cook for many years in Tuskegee, Alabama, and was able to retire. Her deep freezer was always full of great food to eat. When I was a young girl, my grandmother also took care of her daughter, who we affectionally called Ms. Tiny. She was ill most of the time. Her son lived there as well, and my grandmother looked out for my cousin.

My maternal grandmother in New York, who we lived with, was also matriarch with her sons and daughters. She was supportive and always had a warm meal for everyone. She worked at the prestigious Waldorf Astoria Hotel in New York as a housekeeper, and I remember seeing her walking home every evening like clockwork from her train ride. She always had bags in her hand, which meant she had something for us as well as for dinner. She worked hard and purchased a three-family home in New York, and we all lived there on different apartment floors. To this day, our family still lives there as her soul has gone on.

My younger days were filled with independent women, and I did not hear a lot about love. There were successes and failures in relationships that I recall but no significant strides in relational happiness. In a lot of ways, that helped and hurt me as I have been on my journey of single parenting. I would have never thought a decade would pass and I would still be unmarried, but I am grateful that I took this time. I have had significant people in my life over the years, but I have also encountered new pain because of setting expectations too high, too quickly. And I've also been on the other extreme of setting expectations too low, for too long.

I started this chapter off with the question "To Date or Not Date?" I don't claim to have the end all be all answer, but I think I have learned a few things along the way. The first lesson is being a single parent does not make you less of a great pick for someone to date. I allowed myself to be blinded by that myth for some time. The underlying aspect of that was the notion that having children was a liability. Instead, our children are our greatest asset. I recall going on dates and dreading the question of "So you got any kids?" It was like the deal breaker moment in my mind when someone asked me that. I learned to lift my head and say yes, I have two amazing young boys, and I proudly raise them on my own.

Another life lesson – date in the appropriate seasons of life. There were some timeframes where dating just didn't fit in for me. When I was initially divorced, I realized I needed to take some time to get to know myself all over again. A lot was lost over ten years, and I ventured away from the core of myself. Taking the time to regain that self-love and self-trust has been critical in my progression as a single mom. There were points in time where I was just not reliable emotionally! I had days where things seemed to be clear and other days where it just didn't make a whole lot of sense. Why should I put anyone on that roller coaster with me? Also, when my children were younger, I was very particular about who I exposed them too. Children are incredibly delicate at all ages but even more so during the early toddler stages. In those seasons, I sacrificed a lot of my dating desires until the timing was right. Everyone's timing is different, so I do not want to put a time stamp on your timetable. The key is to be aware of your seasons.

Another life lesson – draw a clear line between friendship and romantic interest. I spent a significant amount of years in the cloud of "friendship," hoping for more with the person and losing valuable years. Say what you want and mean it! Friendship is great, but it does not need to be at the expense of your emotions and relationship desires. Friendship cannot be a holding spot for someone who is not ready to commit. I've learned to know my worth and speak up for myself.

Another critical lesson - I needed to desire my wholeness more than wanting a new spouse. My healing needed to be at the forefront of my life. A wedding ring will not cure the areas of my life that I have not dealt with. Issues that you struggle with in singlehood will show up in marriage – unless they are identified and worked on. And even then, there are some areas that we will still struggle with, but awareness will always be a key factor. I now realize that my journey as a single mom was the best thing that ever happened to me. It afforded me the time and opportunity to define me and define my relationship with my sons. Now, as they are growing older, I can distinguish the lines and create space for love in my life. I am a complete package and always will be.

Trust in the Lord with all your heart; do not depend on your own understanding. Seek his will in all you do, and he will show you which path to take.
—Proverbs 3: 5 - 6

One of the most important lessons of all – trust God entirely with everything and seek His will. This scripture always pierces my soul because it admonishes me to trust the Lord with all my heart. You will notice that it does not say "Trust in the Lord with all your mind." It means trust with your heart. The heart is the part of us that carries the "L" word – love. And I cannot just trust God that he will put a meal on my table but refuse to believe God with the love of my heart. And even more, I cannot depend on my understanding because I do not understand at times. I've had the conversation with God – "Lord, you know I'm a good person, you know what I need in my life, but I've failed at love more than once. I don't understand." When I have that real-talk with God, he can show me the areas of my life that I need to continue to work on to be better for Nikki - not just for a relationship.

From the day my counselor asked me that pertinent question, some things were definite. Joshua and Jeremiah did turn five and seven-years-old through the grace of God. And six more years were already added! I was able to finish school and even went back for my master's degree in that timeframe. With God's blessing and favor, I have moved up in my organization with now seventeen years of experience in leadership. I have learned a tremendous amount of lessons during this time, but for someone looking in at my life, one question still lingers – "What about love?" For me, it is a question that I used to ask myself more often at the beginning than I do now because I realize that love is more than just a hot date. Love is about the soul.

You may be wondering, "Nikki, if you found the right person today, what would they be like?" My honest answer is, "They would love me from the soul." I do not have a description of the height he would be, or the body build, or the amount of money. It is not so much about what car or house he has or even his job. The key element that would mean a whole lot to me would be whether he saw my soul. You may be wondering, "Nikki, what are you saying?". Let me explain. The soul is the seat of our emotions. It is the spiritual or immaterial part of us all. It is not something that we can see, but it is a part of us that we must always be aware of. Our souls are the place where we feel and experience within us. It is arguably one of the most valuable aspects of life itself.

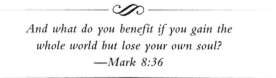

And what do you benefit if you gain the whole world but lose your own soul?
—Mark 8:36

This concept of soul love is someone seeing you from the standpoint of your entire being. Humans are not God, but we can regard each other's feelings and emotions. When someone loves you from the soul, it will cause them to think twice before they hurt you intentionally. They will seek to feed your heart with good things such as encouragement and authenticity because they understand your soul's impact. They take time to know how these aspects drive you as a being. Soul love seeks to remain healthy and releases toxic patterns consciously. Soul love is not perfect, but it regards the fact that everyone is precious in God's sight, understanding we are all fearfully and wonderfully made (Psalms 139:14).

We encounter this type of love first through the Love of God. An absence of love could indicate a lack of God in our lives.

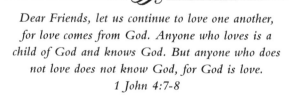

Dear Friends, let us continue to love one another, for love comes from God. Anyone who loves is a child of God and knows God. But anyone who does not love does not know God, for God is love.
1 John 4:7-8

It can become easy to focus on obtaining the love of a man or woman and less focused on embodying the love that you desire. I had to learn how to love when there was no promise of a date or a ring. I had to learn how to love myself. I had to learn how to move away from resentful parenting under challenging times and transform into complete parenting. I've said it before – I have not arrived! I continue to learn life lessons day that guide me along this path of love.

One last major lesson that I will share is a four-letter word that can be painful at times: WAIT. Waiting can be difficult – especially when you are not sure what you are waiting for. I spent a lot of years picturing this knight in shining armor coming to swoop me up (and my babies!) and taking me off into the sunset. This vision is possible from what I have heard! But everyone's life has its' own paths. I had moments where I thought I was on a horse being taken off into the sunset, but there were bumps in the road that knocked me off the horse. I had other times when I saw the horse coming in the sunset ahead but passed me right by – perhaps I wasn't paying enough attention or far enough on the road for the knight and horse to see me.

I spent a lot of years on what seemed the sidelines of life. I had to learn to take the pressure off my children and myself to be perfect in the face of others. I focused on behavior and learning in the home to ensure they would be successful in school and public. I can sit now and look back to see that it paid off. They are growing into well-behaved young men, and they operate themselves accordingly in school and when we are out. It is not perfect days by any means, but what home is? I find a healthy way to navigate the challenges daily through love and attention. I do not know exactly what it all must hold for me, but I know that every lesson has been the fuel to allow me to be healthy and whole in relationships. I've learned to know what I need, be confident in who I am, and trust that there is much happiness ahead. I look forward to what is to come in the days ahead.

Don't' be afraid. I am here to help you. Do
not be dismayed, for I am your God. I will
strengthen you. I will help you. I will uphold
you with my victorious right hand.
—Isaiah 41:10

Single parenting can be one of the loneliest places at times. I've experienced being in a room full of people and feeling the presence of others. Only to leave and get home and feel the tinge of loneliness that comes with this journey. I know what it feels like to come home from work and wish you had someone to tell about your day. And while I have had great people in my life that I could talk to, there is a depth of intimacy I could not get to. Not the intimacy in a bedroom, but the intimacy of allowing someone to see deep into your heart. Loneliness has the effect of erecting walls in our lives. We want the presence of others and yet become afraid to let them fully in emotionally.

Loneliness allowed me to venture to relationships that were comfortable but not necessarily destiny for my life. The emotion of loneliness is real, but it must be identified with an awareness that does not allow it to overtake your life. God knows when you are lonely and even afraid. I had to learn how to sleep lightly because I stood in the position of protecting my home at night. I had to learn how to be observant and discern potential danger for my sons and me. Loneliness can overshadow your ability to see things. Many decisions are made out of loneliness, only to find that it was not the best decision. Feelings of isolation are not limited to those who are single, but it can make you susceptible to it even more.

In those seasons, I have learned to draw on the love of those in my life. I don't put the pressure on my children to replace the absence of a spouse in my life. I refrain from coming home and dumping life's worries on them because they are the only ones there to listen. Instead, I consciously allow them to be children while they still can be. I seek to live a life before them that they would be proud of. I acknowledge when I've missed the mark and ask God for clarity on the next step in my life daily. There is no perfect solution for loneliness, but at those times, I found rest in the fact that God is with me and will take care of me.

I understand that there could be pain that exists because of a breakdown in a relationship that led to the state of singleness. I had to endure years of my internal agony of wondering why I was not good enough to be successful in this area. I want to be transparent because that is the only way that we can move forward. I admit I was angry at times and that I even felt the tinge of depression that fought against my ability to be happy with myself. I had to learn how to feel beautiful again. I looked for my validation to come from a partner and had to come to the stark reality that a partner is human just as I was. Which means they were not perfect. My validation had to come from a higher place. I had to find my peace in the purpose that God had for me on this earth.

My situation was not ideal, but out of it, I was given a blessing — my children. My story is not perfect — but my blessing is perfect. The message is not that you must find a way to be whole again in a relationship. The priority is that you must first declare the blessings that you already have. How can I appreciate something new and beautiful coming into my life, if I cannot first embrace the beauty already there? I must first step back and look at the life that God has allowed me. If it's God's will, the relationship will come knocking at the door — when you are not even looking for it. My worth as a parent is beyond any measure. My freedom starts right there! I was so lost until I embraced this reality in my life.

My two sons are watching and learning from me in this season. It's up to me on what perception I want to leave them with. Is it the "woe is me" mom who sunk into the caves of life and her past? Or is it the "I am strong" mom who stood despite the storm. It doesn't matter how much you have or don't have in this season of your life. What matters is what you have on the inside of you. This is bigger than a date; this is about a lifetime ahead. I sacrificed many years of dating so that I could be present in my journey. This timeline of a decade was not what I planned. But now I realize it was the perfect plan. I needed to be in a different place within me so that I could approach the future differently. This journey is not about how long I will be single. Instead, this journey is about how defined and free I can be until the next season of my life. It's about me looking forward as my sons look to me for direction.

12

The Importance of Family

*Family is the thread of our creation. The thread continues
to be sewn together to create life's beautiful garments.*

There is no way I could write this entire book and not talk about
the importance of family in my life as a single mom. From Super
Grandpa, Cheerleader Mom to Saving Sisters, my life has been filled
with love and family support. I never had a large immediate family.
My family seemed to exist in clusters. I had my mother's family with
Jamaican roots in the New York area. And then I had my father's
family with Southern roots in Alabama. I shifted between both
worlds in my life, leaving me with love for collard greens and curry
chicken! My cultural mix was enriching and made me versatile. My
role as an older sister placed me in a position to grow up quickly. I
recall walking to the corner stores with my little sisters, buying my
food in the afternoons, and watching out for them as we waited for
my mother to come home from work.

Thankfully as I grew older and out of the rebellion stage, I
was able to connect with my mother on a whole new level. We are
so much alike in our character and how we view life. I'm grateful
to have inherited her spirit. My mother became my confidante
early in life, and we still have that relationship to date. My sisters,
although younger than me, grew to be my best friends. When I
became pregnant with my first son, I would not have been able to

get through those days alone. My middle sister Taisha would check on me while I was on bed rest. My hair needed washing, but I could not stand in the shower long. Taisha would come and wash my hair in a bucket of water and then braid it for me until the next time. My younger sister Kima has wisdom beyond her years and has always been able to give me some advice and even correct me if needed! She is our big sister!

Family comes in various shapes and forms in seasons of life. My sister-in-law was also significant support to me during my pregnancies. She took me to doctor visits and checked on me often. My mother-in-law was such a sweet spirit, and she listened whenever I needed someone to talk to. She would always say to me, "Nicole, you are a good person." Those words helped me to remain a woman of character despite my world crashing around me at periods of life. Being on bed rest was one of the most humbling times of life. The longer I stayed in bed, the weaker I seemed to get. I needed help with simple things. Although I had a spouse at the time, my family was still major support for me.

In total, my children spent ninety days in the Neonatal Intensive Care Unit (NICU). My family would come to visit each of my babies. I have pictures of my family reaching their hand in to comfort my little ones in incubators. My mom fasted and prayed faithfully for my two little ones. She would often get off work and drive from New York to come and sit with me in the NICU. My heart was broken a lot in those seasons. For the first few weeks, while Josh was in the NICU, I cried every time I came to see him. My mother would say, "Nikki, don't let Joshua hear you cry all the time." But I could not help it at the time. There is such an emptiness that occurs in a woman when you have your baby, and they are taken right away to intensive care. I did not get to hold him on my chest as I saw in all the movies. It did not go as I imagined – however I was grateful for his life.

As I ventured out on my own to start a new life, I had no clue what God was setting up for me. I had remained close to my father through adulthood. I didn't go for long summers anymore but did visit periodically. Once I got my place, my father started coming to visit the boys and me. Ironically, he was on the brink of early retirement and had some extra time. Joshua and Jeremiah were indeed a handful for Grandpa when he visited. One day while my dad was visiting me at my first apartment there in Newark, NJ, he was sitting on the porch of the house where I lived. I'll never forget looking down at the broken-up concrete that made up the stairs that we used to come into the house. My father was a man of few words, and he did not talk fast, so you just had to stand still and listen.

His words stuck with me, so I remember them clearly to this day from eight years ago. He said to me, "I'm going to help you with the boys, so you don't have to jump into anything just because you need help." It was a few words, but he was saying a lot. He visited a few times, and he saw the strain that I was under alone. And he feared that I would make decisions from a place of need. He wanted me to have a choice. From that day forward, my father committed to helping me with the boys and visited for long stretches to provide additional support at home. He did not do a lot of cooking or domestic chores, but he knew how to watch over the boys and keep them safe, and that was exactly what I needed. He learned how to pick them up from schools and camps and has been actively apart of our lives all these years.

Throughout this whole experience, I made up a new name for my dad – "Super Grandpa." I saw a big "S" on his chest because he saw the need to step in to be there for me at this time of my life. He didn't always agree with my parenting methods as I may have been a little more lenient on the boys than I should have at times. But he understood the delicate balance that I always had in tow as I sought to raise and love them. And he stepped in to provide that support.

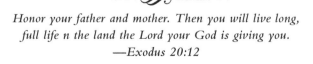

Honor your father and mother. Then you will live long,
full life n the land the Lord your God is giving you.
—Exodus 20:12

My mother has gained a new name as well – "Cheerleader Mom." My mother has continued to speak greatness into my life. Even when I was in the dumps (so it seemed), she would still remind me that there was a calling on my life. That there was so much more for me to do and that I had words to write and say. And I had to live so that I could do it. My mother has been a psychiatric nurse for many years, and she was always keenly aware of any sign of depression or breakdown on the horizon because of her skill. She would remind me that some of her most beautiful patients were women, just like me who, got overwhelmed and had a breaking point. She always said, "Nikki, it's easier to stop the break than it is to come back from the break." Recently, I went through a difficult procedure after fighting the battles of fibroids for some years. My mother was right there by my side. As I entered the operating room, I went into surgery in peace knowing that God was with me, and she would be there when I woke up. She sat in the waiting room, reading her Bible (and nodding from tiredness). It's just who she is and what she does.

As a young girl, I listened to my mother cry at times as she suffered from the pain of divorce. I watched her try to pick up the pieces of her life and make some wrong turns and stumble. But in all of that, she made many right turns that benefitted my sisters and me for a lifetime. At one point, I felt that my role as a single mother was a handed down journey that I had to bear. Yes, some cycles happen in families and appear to be patterned. But I now realize that it was a strength that I inherited from the legacy of women in my family. From the shores of Jamaica to the deep south, I have the infused spirit of women who persevered against all the odds.

Love, Family, and Faith. Those are the key ingredients that have been apart of my life and my greatest blessings. I have learned to embrace the family as it has come into my life. From my church family to work family, I've had the opportunity to connect with awesome people that have impacted my life tremendously. Family relationships are not always perfect. Some periods were struck with breakdowns in family relationships. The key is still the ability to recover.

No matter how large or small a family is, there is something special about family interactions. My sons have a large family on their father's side, and I was always intentional about allowing them to have the open opportunity to bond with both sides of their family. My mother now has seven grandchildren, and it is incredible to watch our family expand through the children. Family comes in many shapes and forms. For me, my church family has also been a significant force in my life during my years of single parenting. During some of my darkest days, my church family continued to impress upon me the need to push forward. My stepmother has been a strong force in my life. She has always been a listening ear and did as much as she could to support me through love over the years.

One of the pitfalls of single parenting has been the temptation to isolate feeling as if others may not understand. There were times I felt that a family member who had a significant other in the home, could not truly realize my struggles. It took so much energy for simple things like getting myself and the boys to a family event dressed and decent. At times, the only adult hug I received may have been during a visit to my mother's house. But even in those times, I learned that family is a thread, and it sews together the fabric of life – always.

13

The Enterprise of Co-Parenting

Our ability to handle change and come to common ground
has a lasting impression on our children. Whether we
are successful or not – they will always remember.

Three years ago, I published a book entitled *Storm Clouds are Passing: Hold on Until Change Comes.* This book was groundbreaking for me because it was the first time that I wrote a non-fiction book with my life interwoven into the story. And it was my first book I wrote after the storm. This book focused on dealing with storms of life and the ability to come out of the storm de-fined and re-fined for the next phase of life. I wrote this book in a period and stage where I was finally able to say, "It's Ok" to my life circumstances. I had come to a place of peace in my life regarding my divorce and my plight as a single mom. I had the opportunity to focus on the biblical hero Job, who weathered a significant storm and did not sin against God.

The moral of the entire story is finding the ability not to lose the core of who you are in the storm. Have you ever known someone before they went through a difficult situation, and they seem the exact opposite when it is all said and done? There is a transition that can happen in the storm that either makes you better or bitter. I chose to come out of the storm without the bitterness that would crowd out the rest of my life. Let me be real with you – it was not an overnight process. I went through an array of feelings after divorce. I climbed into a lot of caves of self-pity to nurture the wounds – while I was still parenting. But Joshua and Jeremiah were the force in my life that always pushed me to continue to show up. I knew that I couldn't sink into depression and close the blinds and stop working. If I did that, how would they eat! It was just that simple for me on some days. You learn to use whatever motivates you to keep going forward.

This chapter is super important because co-parenting can be one of the most treacherous areas for single parenting after a relationship breakdown. How we handle co-parenting can define the health of our children in their current years and beyond. You notice that I did not say the health of the adults necessarily. In cases where there are abuse and danger, it does become more about the health of the adult and the child as well. However, when possible, without those mitigating factors, we must see the co-parenting task as a joint effort between two adults focused on the health of the children.

My children are backpack kids. They pack up a bag on a Friday with just enough to last till Sunday and give me hugs. We have done this for many years. I used to pack the weekend bags with bottles, and now they pack their bags on their own. Their dad used to leave with baby bags, and now he picks up two tall young men with backpacks. There are times that my heart sinks as I watch them pack up. I know their time with their father is essential, but I miss them as well. But I understand my need to rest and recharge.

We use the term co-parenting to refer to the joint effort of two parents. I was intrigued by the Wikipedia definition of co-parenting that defines it as "an enterprise undertaken by two or more adults who together take on the socialization, care, and upbringing of children for whom they share responsibility" (https://en.wikipedia. org/wiki/Coparenting). The word enterprise stuck with me because we should see it that way. It is an effort that requires strategic focus and energy to ensure it is successful.

When you are the single custodial parent, it can feel lopsided when you balance out all the weight of the day-to-day. I am responsible for breakfast, getting them off to school, dinner when they get home, and then tucking them in at night. Much of their well-being is my responsibility. However, I've learned that allowing the other parent to be a part when possible helps to balance out the load. Even if it is two or three weekends a month – it is a valuable time for me to recharge for the other days of the month.

My situation has transformed tremendously over the years, and I am proud of how Joshua & Jeremiah's dad and I co-parent. It took time to grow it and develop those critical boundaries. When Joshua and Jeremiah were younger, I did not realize how much they would need a male figure. With my father being there with me most of the time, it helped to fill some of that space. But there was a light that lit up in their eyes when their daddy arrived that I didn't see anywhere else. And I promised myself that I would not allow that light to go out in their eyes for their dad. He is an upstanding God-fearing man, veteran to our country, stems from a great family, and embodies great morals. Why would I take that opportunity away from my young men to embrace those characteristics about their father?

Even in the toughest years when we did not agree, I never withheld my sons from spending time with their father. I was careful to find the balance between not forcing it either. I always wanted it to be mutual love and bond between them that they could carry for the rest of their lives with their father. After all, my mother had done the same for me. When their dad remarried many years ago, they gained a great stepmom and three brothers, two of which were in the same age range. They are like brothers matched in heaven. It is undeniable that they were meant to know each other as brothers and friends, and I look forward to them growing up together as young men.

Someone may be saying, "I'm just not there." And that is ok. It comes in stages and phases. My advice would be to focus on getting there. I will tell you why this is important. Forgiveness is one of the greatest keys we can ever experience on this earth. The core of forgiveness does not always unlock the heart of someone else, but it will forever open your own heart. I had to learn to forgive, and it had to start with forgiving myself. I could not allow the circumstances of my broken marriage to dictate how we would ultimately raise the children. I knew my intimate relationship ended with my husband, but the connection to parent our children remains for a lifetime.

I used to feel guilty when my children packed their bags to venture off with their dad. I felt like I failed them in some way, and we could have done this differently. But every moment that I allowed those feelings to stagger in my soul – it was a moment lost to be able to embrace the present and make the best of where I was. I realized that dwelling on the past was crippling my future, and God intended to do something new and great in my life.

For I am about to do something new. See I have already begun! Do you not see it? I will make a pathway through the wilderness. I will create rivers in the dry wasteland.
—Isaiah 43: 18 - 19

In this scripture, God promises the captives that they will experience victory. In earlier verses in this chapter, God reminds them of all he has done for them. He opened the way through waters, which was a great thing. But God tells them that I am getting ready to do something even greater in your life. I'm getting ready to create new pathways through those wilderness periods. I am a living witness that God can take a dry wasteland in your life and allow rivers of blessings to flow through it. As I embraced faith in my life, it allowed me to embrace forgiveness, and forgiveness allowed me to release. I released myself from the bonds of my past regrets. The reality was I only have this moment. The last moment in which you read the prior sentence has already moved on. Your time is now!

Successful Co-parenting involves the understanding that two people are in something together for the higher benefit. When possible, it should be embraced. Wikipedia's definition also states that co-parents may include a variety of configurations, including a parent and another adult relative. It takes a village, and therefore, co-parenting may come in the form of someone other than the biological parent. It could be a stepparent or an uncle, or even a close friend. The objective is that the focus of the relationship is solely the child. Separation of the family is not an easy event for a child. I sit and observe my sons at times, and I pray for their souls and their ability to have successful relationships. While it may not cure all ills, I believe co-parenting as an enterprise can set the stage for success. I wanted to ensure I included this in my book because it may be helpful to someone.

I recently made one of the boldest moves in my life – all for the sake of co-parenting. A few years back, my sons, their dad, and I sat down to have dinner and a real-life discussion. It was a Thursday evening, and we were at a Portuguese restaurant in downtown Newark, New Jersey – the heart of the Portuguese district. This restaurant was one of our favorites. It was known for cooking the meats over an open fire there in the restaurant. Each platter came with sinful portions of rice and French fries. It was close to my job at the time, and I went there often and brought food home for the boys from there. I could not lose much weight during those years.

We chose this restaurant filled with comfort food to have a tough conversation with our sons. Through a series of events, their dad was leaving New Jersey and moving to North Carolina. He offered the boys to go with him, and he was willing to take full responsibility to raise them, and then visit me in the summers. Since the boys were old enough, we wanted them to have a decision on the matter. Of course, I was not too happy with this upcoming arrangement, but I always kept the well-being of the boys in mind, so I thought to give them some time to talk about it with us was vital. They had already known about this upcoming change for some months by then. It was down to the wire and almost time for him to go. I could see the pain in his eyes as he talked to Joshua and Jeremiah about his desire to take them with him. It's as if he knew they would decide to stay in New Jersey with me upfront.

After we ate, the big question landed on the table with the weight of its existence "Boys, do you want to go to North Carolina or stay in New Jersey with Mommy?" They looked at their dad and said, "We are staying with Mommy." With his heart heavy, he reassured them that it was the right decision and that we would make the best of this situation. We turned our conversation towards the fun Southern summers ahead for the boys. I walked out of the restaurant with this sinking feeling. In retrospect, I am grateful to his wife, who was always an advocate for ensuring we had those critical moments together as a co-parenting unit. To this day, she remains a positive relationship in my life.

For the next two weeks after that meeting, I felt this overwhelming sadness. But it wasn't my own. I had this strong innate motherly instinct that I was carrying the burden of sadness for my sons. As they went along with their days, I spent private time crying the tears they did not need to shed. I wanted to carry it so they wouldn't have to. Life was getting ready to change for them – and me. After their dad's relocation, we moved towards holidays and summers, and they enjoyed those times. I cried when I dropped them off to him, and then he cried when I picked them up. We did our best to share them as we could.

Then a shift occurred two years ago in my life that seemed to change the course forever. Through a series of miraculous God created events, and after working with my company for over fifteen years, I was offered an opportunity for advancement in North Carolina. A few weeks later, we were living in the same state as their father, and they reunited once again. I cannot pretend that this was an easy decision for me. I knew that it would cause some to say that I was following him. I knew it would be hard to leave my family behind. But I also knew I was ready for a change in a significant way. The offer given by my company was one that I could not refuse. Every detail was taken care of for my relocation, and I became a part of a new work family that I will adore forever.

My career growth has been astronomical upon this move, and I was able to build a home for my sons – something I desired for so many years. There were and still are some difficult days as we have made this transition over the past year. New job, new place, new people. But I take this opportunity to find the new "me" as well. The proximity and engagement of their father afforded me some ability to venture out on some of my life passions and travel desires. I have not yet even tapped the surface!

Through all of this, I learned that my sons needed their father. And yes, I believe God will allow new love in my life that will serve as a father figure. My benefit is I am not shopping for a replacement father in a man, only a supplemental benefit to the great male figures they already have in their life. It allows me to approach relationships at a healthy level. Life affords us the ability to continue to adjust as we go along the way. Co-parenting is one of those adjustments, and I pray my sons will always remember my advocacy. I salute the men and women around this world who make a concentrated effort to raise their children together – whether in the same household or separate. I salute those who may not have the option to co-parent, but they allow others to step in and help when needed so they can stay the course. In the end, it is all about our children, our blessings.

And now, dear brothers and sisters, one final thing.
Fix your thoughts on what is true, and honorable,
and right, and pure, and lovely, and admirable. Think
about things that are excellent and worthy and praise.
—Philippians 4:8

A key area in any situation is the thought processes attached to it. To co-parent successfully, I had to learn to disassociate some of my personal feelings from the situation so that I could allow what was most valuable to come to the surface. There is value to the enterprise of co-parenting, and it is a crucial family dynamic in our society. We recently needed to meet with Joshua's team of teachers to discuss how he was doing in his classes. Although it was clear that we were not married, we had a powerful effect on us coming to the meeting as a team. We were "Team Joshua," and that is what mattered at that moment. We sat down to talk, and Joshua's dad had his paper and pencil ready to take notes. I offered him the opportunity to speak first as his father. I chimed in on the health aspect of Joshua's life because that is what I am familiar with. Overall, we were on the same page, and at the end of the meeting, we walked away with a plan to help Joshua as a team. Any disagreement we had on strategy was held until we were outside of the school and could regroup.

This is an example of how the enterprise of co-parenting can be valuable when it is available. All situations do not allow for that. But we also need to ensure that we have not created our barriers to this type of interaction. At times, my sons will ask for their stepbrothers to come over and stay for a weekend with us. I now have been allowed to get to know these young men as well, and they are apart of our family structure when they come over. I embrace the chance to shine a light in their lives each chance I get. They affectionately call me "Auntie," and that is an honor that they can see my heart and know that I mean them well – even as an aunt would. I've tried not to let my past inhibit me from not taking advantage of the bright future. I am humbled that their mom entrusts me with her precious blessings physically as well as spiritually. It's not uncommon to see me with all four boys, taking them to church, out for lunch, or to play in the park. My co-parenting enterprise extends beyond only my children – and into the lives of other children as well.

How we show up in the most challenging moments is what our children will remember most. One day, Jeremiah asked me, "Mommy, are you a kind person?" I looked over at him to see where he was going with that. Jeremiah is a very intuitive child, and when he speaks – it's important to listen! I replied, "Jeremiah, I think I am kind. I want to be kind." He looked back at me and said, "Mommy, you are a kind person." See, he asked me first to determine if I was aware of my characteristic and then affirmed it with his interpretation. Kindness is not something that you can write a playbook on and tell children how to do. It's something that they must see and then adopt – it's inherent in the heart of the individual. I believe Jeremiah sees me as kind, based on how I have handled the relationships in my life. It's not about giving or sharing tangible items – but it's the emotional giving and sharing that displays the kindness as well. Whatever things are true, honorable, right, and loving – think on those things.

14

A Mother's Love

*A mother's love is unexplainable. It is a personal gift
given to a woman by God for all who will accept it.*

It has been an absolute joy to write this book. It allowed me to have
the humbling opportunity of sharing some of my life stories with
lessons I learned and inspiring moments. As I came to this chapter,
I did not initially know what the last chapter of the book would be.
I wondered how I could end. Reality is I did not want it to end!
But I know that this work is completing to create space for the next
task that God has laid on my heart. Without any specifics, I decided
that Memoir # 14 would be the last chapter. And I would take this
chapter to talk about a mother's love. It is not meant to exclude
fathers in any way! A father's love is just as powerful. But since this
is my memoir, I am writing from my perspective.

A mother's love is a vital part of our children's lives. Some
children may not have their mothers living here on this earth,
or through circumstances, the love of their mother is or was not
available to them. And for those children, my heart breaks because
there is a special ingredient in our love that I believe was God-
ordained. A mother's love is not perfect. I am not perfect each day
as I walk this parenting journey. There are evenings that I end the
day and wish I did or said something differently. But love is the

instrument that allows me to remain conscious and aware of how my love is displayed to my children.

In the beginning, I shared the story of how I fought hard for my two sons – first to come into this world, then as they grew. I did not have a smooth start to their lives, and I watched them endure pain through surgeries and illnesses. My love for them made me cry, wishing I could bear the pain for them. My love for them can even cause me to cry when I think about the world and challenges that lay ahead of them. I am raising two African American boys who will become young men, and they may face the stigma and racism that has existed in our world – simply because of the color of their skin. My mother's love makes me find ways to shelter them from that possibility if I can. At the same time, I prepare them carefully for the opportunities of what lies ahead.

Mother's love prevents you from blaming your children for your mishaps in life. They will never be the cause of me being a single mother. Instead, they are the joy in my life that has allowed me to walk this journey of single parenthood with pride. Each day that we dwell here together on this earth is a precious day that I can never remake again – all I have is my memory. My love for them charges me to maximize the moments with them as best as I can. My love for them continuously challenges me to teach them the right way to go as often as possible.

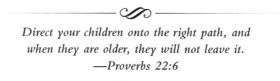

Direct your children onto the right path, and
when they are older, they will not leave it.
—Proverbs 22:6

My lineage is made up of women who made sacrifices on both my maternal and paternal side of the family. Although I cannot recall all my experiences with them, I know that I walk on the legacy of mothers who endured all to make way for others. My maternal grandmother worked hard to buy a home as an immigrant that our family can still dwell in today. My paternal grandmother led an example of strength and love as she raised her children on her own in widowhood – never once looking back. I have met so many great parents along my way in this life who balance careers and family life – and never forget the element of love. I salute them all – the mothers and fathers I know, the mothers and fathers I am destined to meet, and the mothers and fathers I will never meet, but we connect through this writing.

There is a story in the book of Kings in the Bible (1 Kings 3:16 -28) that gives the account of two women who both had newborns and dwelled together. On the third night, one of the women laid on her child mistakenly in her sleep, and the child died overnight. She realized this in the middle of the night and proceeded to switch the baby, who was no longer living with the other woman's living child. When the other woman woke up that morning, she discovered the child on her bosom was no longer living. I can't imagine the grief she felt looking down at the baby. She looked closely at the baby and realized that the child was not hers. Although the children may have looked similar, there was a distinction about her child in her eyes. I can be out in a room full of kids, but when one of my sons calls out "Mommy!", I distinctly know their sound and their voice. Even in a room full of boys, I can pick my two sons out right away because all my senses are keenly aware of them.

As this story continues, the women proceeded to argue regarding whose child each was – the living child or the baby who passed away. Because of this dispute, they stood before King Solomon, who was known for great wisdom. Something happened at this moment, which stunned me the first time I initially read it. The King listened intently to both women's arguments. I can only imagine them screaming to make their case – they were both brokenhearted and needed intervention. They may have been the best of friends before, but at this moment, it was about making a case for who's baby was still living. The King asked for a sword and proceeded to make the declaration that the living child would be divided in two since they both could not agree and could both have half of the child.

The idea of that happening was startling! But the King had

a plan – he wanted to reveal the pure heart of a mother. One woman immediately said, "No, please don't hurt the child! She can have him – just let him live!" At that moment, this woman no longer cared about making her case. Her heart cry was for the safety and well-being of the baby first. She was willing to sacrifice her motherhood so he could live. The King observed the reactions of the second woman who surprisingly did not care what happened to the living child. I imagine her grief of losing her child was so deep at that moment. In the end, the King ordered the child to be given to the woman who pleaded for the child's life with these written words – "She is his mother!" (1 Kings 3:27). When people heard about this, they were in awe of the wisdom of King Solomon. I have always been in awe of this account as well.

This demonstration was meant to display the sacrificial love of a mother. Children are gifts from God, on loan to us here on earth. The title of this book is "My Greatest Blessings." I have a picture with my sons that has the same words as a reminder. The word blessing relates to a beneficial thing for which one is grateful-something that brings well-being. God has allowed me to receive many benefits here on this earth. But my greatest blessings are the two children that I have been graced with love and parent here on earth. I wanted to write this from the single parent perspective because I felt the strong need to capture this chapter of my life and hopefully inspire someone else as they journey through it as well. I also wanted to have a legacy that my sons can look back on when they are older. It is an imprint of my heart for this journey of raising them and appreciating what they mean to me. Oh, how they have blessed me – and I hope to continue to be a blessing to them. One day, one moment at a time. Embrace your blessings!

Joshua and Jeremiah,
You will always be MY GREATEST BLESSINGS!

TIME OF REFLECTION

Reflection is the ability to look into the water and
see ourselves through a different lens. Then to be
able to reach into the water and be refreshed.

The next few pages present the opportunity to reflect on the book's different aspects as you read along by chapter or at the end. Feel free to use these questions to foster internal or group discussion. These questions are not limited to parenting but can be utilized by all readers. Grab a journal and write down your thoughts. Spend time with it and go as deep as you need to be refreshed. There are five specific questions in each chapter, but the depth can lead you into more questions. Write down your questions and challenge yourself to go deeper and experience the blessings that God has intended for you.

The objective of this book is not only to share my experiences but also to transform the dynamic of how someone may have viewed life prior. There may be a single mom, who now will emphasize the joy of parenting, rather than her marital status. There may be married parents who decide to view their parenting through a different life as well. And then someone may read this who is not a parent, but they have found nuggets of information to push them ahead into the next phase of life. I hope the times of reflection over the next few pages are meaningful to you.

Memoir # 1 – Reflection Questions

One More Epi!

1. Take time to identify the miraculous moments in your life and how it made you feel?

2. Have you ever asked for a miracle in your life and then had to walk through a difficult journey to see it fulfilled?

3. Nikki shares her "One More Epi" experience in the delivery room. What are your "One More Epi" experiences in your life?

4. How have you learned to cope with difficult seasons in your life?

5. What difficulties in parenting have you overcome and can share a testimony of God's strength in your life?

Memoir # 2 – Reflection Questions

God Did it Again

1. We all experience times where we are given a second chance. What are those moments in your life that you can identify?

2. Sometimes difficult decisions are made during delicate times. Has this ever occurred in your life?

3. Nikki describes the balancing act of having two premature babies. What responsibilities in your life have stretched you?

4. What tools and tactics have you used to cope during times you felt stretch?

5. Parenting comes with responsibility but also with great joy. How can you continue to capture the moments along the way?

Memoir # 3 – Reflection Questions

Why Your Story is Important

1. What is your story? Take time to write it down and narrate from your point of view.

2. What stigmas and/or stereotypes do you believe have shaped how you view your own story?

3. What parts of your story do you need to re-vise and re-tell? Take the time to start to do this now.

4. How is your view of life changing through the points mentioned in this chapter?

5. How can you foster real change and transformation in your life, and what will it look like?

Memoir # 4 – Reflection Questions

Organize, Organize, and Trust

1. Organizing has been primarily thought to be personality driven. What is your view of organization in your own life?

2. As a single parent, Nikki describes how organization has benefited her. What are the tactics you already have or can put in place to be more organized?

3. Organization extends beyond physical organization of tasks. It extends to our thought processes. Do you feel organized in your thoughts and emotions? If not, spend time identifying why.

4. How are you organizing and planning for the future? Is there more you need to do?

5. Organization is a useful tool, but the element of trust in God must also be inherent. Take time to meditate and write about the level of trust in your life.

Memoir # 5 – Reflection Questions

4 a.m. Study Sessions

1. Are there any dreams you have placed on hold throughout your life? Why did you put them on hold?

2. What are some of your dreams and aspirations? What do you look forward to?

3. It is often said that delay does not mean denial. What delays have you experienced, and how can you push past those delays?

4. At the end of the chapter, Nikki talks about lifting her hands as a symbolism of letting go of things that may have held her back. What are some things you can let go of as you lift your own hands?

5. Sometimes we may feel as if we missed the opportunities afforded to us in life. How can you pick up the pieces right from where you are and begin again?

Memoir # 6 – Reflection Questions

Rest for the Weary

1. At the start of the chapter, it says, "Rest is our friend who we sometimes promise we will see soon when the time is right." If rest is a friend, how would you describe your relationship? Is it something you know well or neglect?

2. Rest is beyond the act of sleeping at night. What other ways can we "rest" in our lives?

3. Nikki makes the point that to withstand for the future; she must rest now. What do you look forward to in the future? What adjustments can you make now to meet to give you the best opportunity for the future?

4. What do you say "YES" to emotionally in your life that can cause you to be drained and unfulfilled?

5. What strategies can you put in place to ensure you get the proper rest so you can be healthy and whole?

Memoir # 7 – Reflection Questions

Corporate Ladder in One Hand – Baby in Other

1. Pursuing a career and being a parent is not an easy task. What sacrifices have you had to make in your life as you attempted to balance both worlds?

2. What is the most essential aspect of ensuring your family life is not neglected while still ensuring to pursue your vocation?

3. Do you know what your career desire is, or have you just been getting by with the best you can find for the season you are in? How can you activate your faith to pursue your dreams?

4. When children are young, they don't always understand the balancing act of career and home. How can we give them the proper attention despite our efforts?

5. How do we utilize our lives to demonstrate that parents are just as capable in the workplace? How can we lead by example?

Memoir # 8 – Reflection Questions

EBA – Finding "You" with all the balls in the air

1. In this chapter, Nikki lays out key words from the definition of "balance." What words stuck out to you as read them?

2. What are the key areas that you find yourself trying to balance daily?

3. Why do you think we sometimes lose ourselves as we seek to juggle all the balls of responsibility?

4. How does living an unbalanced life affect our physical and emotional well-being?

5. What promises can you make to yourself to ensure you can remain focused on you during times of stress? What self-care tactics can you put in place?

Memoir # 9 – Reflection Questions

When the Money is Funny

1. Recall times when the "money was funny" and how you got through those times.

2. Financial worries can burden single-parent families or any family model. How can we guard against letting the fear of lack of finances dominate our parenting life?

3. Nikki shares her experience of trying to go to Disney World when she was in a "Chuck E Cheese" season. Do you find yourself ever trying to overcompensate financially?

4. Matthew 6:25 – 27 admonishes us not to worry, but to trust in our Heavenly Father. How can you find more ways to worry less and grow trust?

5. What can we teach our children about finances early on in life to ensure they can manage money well regardless of their situations?

"Faith - Not Fiction"

1. At the start of the chapter, it states, "When Faith and Hope intersect, it creates the road to destiny." What does this statement mean to you?

2. How has faith played a role in your life from childhood until the present?

3. What are some ways to increase your faith as a parent, and how can it impact your children?

4. There are times where we all struggle with having faith during difficult times in our lives. Reflect on some of those times and identify areas you are grateful for despite the difficulty.

5. How can we teach our younger generations through putting in place "memorial stones" to remind them of what God has done for us?

Memoir # 11 – Reflection Questions

"To Date or Not to Date...That is the Question"

1. What comes to mind as you think about the topic of dating and single parenting? What feelings does it trigger within you?

2. What have you found to be the greatest challenge of being a single parent and dating?

3. Has this chapter helped to confirm or change some of your perception about dating? If so, what specifically has touched home with you?

4. What are the challenges that parents can face when trying to date? What does a successful relationship look like?

5. What areas in your past may need to be resolved before you attempt to have a successful relationship?

Memoir # 12 – Reflection Questions

The Importance of Family

1. How do you define family and what are some of your childhood memories of a family? How has that played out in your life as an adult?

2. In the busyness of our world, family connections can dwindle. How can we consciously cultivate those relationships to keep them alive?

3. Nikki shares that there was extended family in her life who encouraged her during difficult times. Who are people who have been like family in your life, and how did they impact you?

4. Children come into the world without bias as it relates to their families. How can we foster those relationships in the lives of our children and create safe spaces for them to grow in love?

5. Write down some people in your family who you have not spoken with for a while and make a note to reach out with a phone call or even to send a card to let them know you are thinking of them.

Memoir # 13 – Reflection Questions

The Enterprise of Co-Parenting

1. Co-parenting offers a valuable solution for parents to agree on the care of a child. Why do you think there has been an issue with this at times, and what are some barriers?

2. What are strategies that can be put in place to co-parent on essential decisions like holidays and schools?

3. Co-parenting after divorce can be healthy for the child but also may create new feelings of insecurity as the child has to share time between both parents. How can each parent make the child(ren) feel secure despite the separate homes?

4. All situations are not peaceful and conducive to single parenting. What are some red flags, and how can we address those red flags?

5. Personal feelings due to relational breakdown can be a barrier to effective co-parenting. If you are experiencing this, identify those feelings and come up with a plan for how you will address those feelings.

Memoir # 14 – Reflection Questions

A Mother's Love

1. This chapter sums up the entire memoir – A mother's love. Whether you are a mother or not, we all have experienced the love of our mothers. Take some time to write about what a mother's love means to you.

2. Nikki shares about the sacrificial aspect of a mother's love. What have you sacrificed as a mother, or what has your mother sacrificed for you? Express your gratitude for those areas.

3. Nikki's intent for writing this book was to highlight the blessing of being a single mom. What do you walk away with as it relates to Nikki's message?

4. A mother's love prevents you from blaming your children for mishaps in your life. How can we show our children how much we love them, even in difficult times?

5. Nikki ends this chapter with a declaration to her sons that they are her greatest blessings. Write down and speak out the names of those who are your greatest blessings in your life.

ABOUT THE AUTHOR

Nikki Henderson can be described as "a woman after God's own heart." She lives through God's remarkable testimony in her life of forgiveness and restoration. Since her teenage years, Nikki has served in ministry in praise and worship, youth ministry, women's ministry, preaching, and teaching the Word of God. Nikki believes that God has called her to the brokenhearted and to share a message of God's love and restoration. Nikki desires to empower everyone she encounters to walk in their purpose every day, even in difficult times. Nikki is a worshipper at heart and was granted the opportunity to be a part of a European Tour with The Glory Gospel Singers to spread God's message of Salvation and love through music.

This call to ministry and her life journey inspired her to publish her first book entitled *Moments with God: Short Stories for the Soul of a Woman* in 2014, and she released her second book, *Storm Clouds are Passing: Hold On Until Change Comes* in August 2017. Throughout the years, God has opened the doors for Nikki to speak at Women, Youth, and Prayer conferences to spread God's message of hope and healing. Nikki has taken Biblical courses to further her understanding of God's Word at Nyack College and the Zarephath Bible Institute.

Nikki earned her Bachelor of Business Administration at Thomas Edison University. Determined to stay on the journey, Nikki has also pursued and completed a master's degree in Business Administration (MBA) at the University of Mount Olive. Nikki has over 17 years of leadership experience in Corporate America, including coaching and strategy development and implementation.

Nikki currently resides in North Carolina with her two sons, Joshua, and Jeremiah. Both born at 27 and 30 weeks, Nikki has personally experienced the grace of God on her journey through the premature birth of her sons. Nikki's heart desire is to be all that God has called her to be and serve in love, humility, and gratitude.

Nikki would love to hear from you. Feel free to send an email to Nhenderson76@outlook.com. You can also find Nikki Henderson on social media platforms to connect.

CPSIA information can be obtained
at www.ICGtesting.com
Printed in the USA
BVHW031126250620
582309BV00004B/39/J